CODING
FOR
BEGINNERS
USING
PYTHON

Written by:
Louie Stowell
with Rosie Dickins

Illustrated by: John Devolle

Designed by: Matt Preston

Coding consultants:
Sean Oxspring &
Ben Woodhall

CONTENTS

CHAMPION PROGRAMMER

USBORNE QUICKLINKS

You can find links to useful Python websites and extra information about downloading and using Python at the **Usborne Quicklinks** website at **www.usborne.com/quicklinks**.

(See page 85.)

WHAT IS CODING?

Coding means writing instructions for computers, and a finished set of instructions is known as a program. Computer programs control everything from smartphones to space rockets.

SPEAKING THE RIGHT LANGUAGE

To write a computer program, you have to break down all your instructions into clear, simple steps and express them in a language that a computer can understand.

⚠ **WARNING** ⚠

Computers follow instructions blindly – they can't think for themselves. So everything must be spelled out clearly, leaving nothing out.

WHAT'S A COMPUTER LANGUAGE?

Computer languages are like human languages, but with fewer words and very precise rules about how to use them.

Python is a *text-based* computer language, which means it's made up of words, numbers and symbols (such as * and =).

```
Python 3.5.1 Shell                    _ □ ✕
File  Edit  Shell  Debug  Options  Window  Help
>>> print ("Hello world!")
```

This is a sample of Python code. You can find out what it does on page 7.

Although the logo for the Python language is a snake, it's actually named after a classic British comedy group, Monty Python.

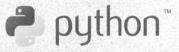

python™

WHY CHOOSE PYTHON?

Python is one of the most popular computer languages and it's very concise – that is, you don't need to type much in order to create programs that do a lot.

Many big organizations such as Google, NASA and YouTube use it to build their programs. You can use it to control hobby computers, too, such as the BBC micro:bit and the Rasberry Pi.

LET'S GET SSSTARTED

GETTING STARTED

You'll need a laptop or desktop computer to run Python. Turn to page 86, or go to **www.usborne.com/quicklinks** and type in 'python', for instructions on how to find Python on your computer, or download it for free if you don't have it already.

Online, you will also find links to other useful coding resources and Python files containing finished, working code for the programs in this book.

Please follow the safety guidelines at the **Usborne Quicklinks** website when using the internet.

WHAT YOU'LL FIND IN THIS BOOK

This book will show you how to make the most of Python with all sorts of projects, from writing your first program to creating your own games.

Everything is broken down into short, easy-to-follow steps, and there's a glossary at the back with definitions of useful words.

Look out for yellow boxes with **TIPS** on using **PYTHON**.

The blue boxes explain **KEY IDEAS** about coding in general.

STARTING PYTHON

Once you've got Python on your machine, you can start creating programs immediately.

IDLE

When you download Python, you also get a program called **IDLE** that helps you write, edit and save your code. Not all Python coders use **IDLE**, but it's a good place to start.

ON WINDOWS®

To open **IDLE** on a Windows® computer, open the 'Start Menu', go to 'All Programs', then select the Python folder and click on IDLE.

ON A MAC®

The process is very similar on a Mac® computer. Open 'Finder', then 'Applications', then the Python folder, and click on IDLE.

THE SHELL WINDOW

The window that pops up when you open IDLE is known as the **Shell window**. It looks like this on a Windows® computer:

Python can look slightly different on different computers, but it works in the same way.

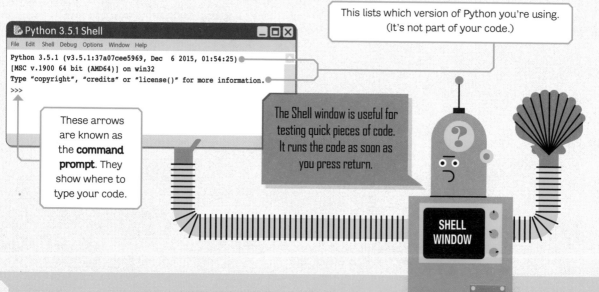

Turn to page 86 to find out about downloading Python if you don't have it already.

This lists which version of Python you're using. (It's not part of your code.)

```
Python 3.5.1 Shell
File  Edit  Shell  Debug  Options  Window  Help
Python 3.5.1 (v3.5.1:37a07cee5969, Dec  6 2015, 01:54:25)
[MSC v.1900 64 bit (AMD64)] on win32
Type "copyright", "credits" or "license()" for more information.
>>>
```

These arrows are known as the **command prompt**. They show where to type your code.

The Shell window is useful for testing quick pieces of code. It runs the code as soon as you press return.

SHELL WINDOW

6

SAY HELLO

It's traditional in the programming world to make the computer say 'Hello world!' with your very first piece of code. In Python, this is very simple.

1. Open the Shell window.

2. Type this (minus the **command prompt** arrows):

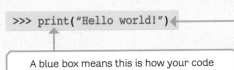
```
>>> print("Hello world!")
```

Make sure you copy this exactly, including the punctuation.

A blue box means this is how your code will look on screen. (You'll find out what the text colours mean on page 13.)

3. Press return. You should see this:

```
Hello world!
```

A green box means this is what you will get when you *run* the program.

DID IT WORK?

If you make a mistake in your code, you'll usually get a red error message. It might look like this:

```
SyntaxError: invalid syntax
```

If that happens, carefully re-type the code on the next line, checking that what you type matches this *exactly*:

This probably means you've typed something wrong. Check your spelling, punctuation and capital letters.

```
>>> print("Hello world!")
```

Lower case 'p'

Open and close quote marks

Press return to run the code.

FUNCTIONS

In Python, the command **print()** is a **function** – essentially a mini, pre-written program. To make it run, all you need to do is type the word. The **print()** function makes the computer show whatever is in the brackets on screen.

HELLO

Congratulations, you've written your first Python program. (The world says 'hello' back, by the way.)

SYNTAX

So the computer can understand your code, you have to spell everything correctly and lay it out in the right way. The combination of spelling, punctuation and layout is called **syntax**.

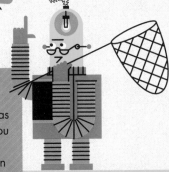

DEBUGGING

Fixing errors in code is known as **debugging**. Don't worry if you make mistakes; all coders do. (That's why they need their own word for fixing them.)

SAVING YOUR CODE

The Shell window is great for testing short pieces of code, but it won't let you *save* anything.

To save your code so you can run it again or edit it later, you need to use something called the **Code window**.

1. Click on **File** (at the top) to open the **File menu**. Select 'New File' and a Code window labelled 'Untitled' will pop up, like this.

2. Click on **File** at the top of the Code window and select 'Save As'. Enter a name you'll remember, with **.py** at the end, then click 'Save'.

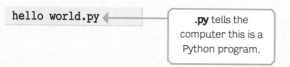

.py tells the computer this is a Python program.

3. Type in the text below, just as you did before:

```
print("Hello world!")
```

The Code window has no command prompt arrows.

4. Click on **File** again, and select 'Save'.

5. Now click on **Run** and select 'Run Module' from the drop-down menu (**module** here means a Python file.)

6. The Shell window should pop up and the words 'Hello world!' should appear.

COMPUTERS AREN'T CLEVER

Computers can't think for themselves, so even tiny mistakes confuse them. Just typing a lower case letter instead of a capital will stop a computer from recognizing a word.

I've been programmed to know that a *lion* is dangerous.

But that's a *Lion*, so I'm fine!

Lion

Python files are automatically saved in the same folder as the Python program.

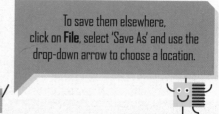

To save them elsewhere, click on **File**, select 'Save As' and use the drop-down arrow to choose a location.

PLAYING WITH NUMBERS

Python makes it easy to do maths.
In the Shell window, you just type in a question
and press return for the answer.

ADDING UP

Open the Shell window and type this:

```
>>> 2 + 2
```

Then press return. You should see the answer:

```
4
```

SUBTRACTING (AND MORE)

If you want to subtract, use the – symbol,
like this:

```
>>> 2 - 2
```

To multiply, use the * symbol:

```
>>> 2 * 2
```

To divide, use the / symbol:

```
>>> 2 / 2
```

In Python, you don't use the = symbol for
doing maths. That symbol has another
use. Turn the page to find out more.

OPERATORS

Symbols like **+** or **–** are known as **operators** in
Python. Here are some common maths operators:

+ means add

– means subtract, or take away

∗ means multiply

/ means divide

Why do I need Python to do maths?
I have a calculator for that.

Python can handle far more
complicated calculations
than a calculator, and use
the answers to do things
such as keeping track of
game scores.

In maths, you use **x** for multiply
and **÷** for divide.
But **÷** isn't on most keyboards,
and **x** looks like a letter.
So coders use **∗** and **/** instead.

VARIABLES

A **variable** is like a labelled box that stores information. You can change this information, but the label stays the same.

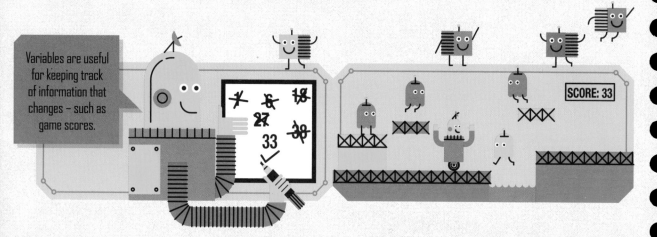

Variables are useful for keeping track of information that changes – such as game scores.

SCORE: 33

HOW TO CREATE A VARIABLE

To tell the computer what you want your variable to be, you use the = sign. This is called *assigning a value to the variable*. It's very simple. Here's an example, using bananas.

1. Open the Shell window.

2. Type in the following:

```
>>> bananas = 5
```

Note: you won't see anything happen. The computer just stores the information to use later.

You have now created a variable called 'bananas' and given it a **value** of 5.

NAMING VARIABLES

You can give a variable any name you like, as long as it doesn't contain spaces or certain special characters or 'keywords' that already mean something in Python. (You'll know if you accidentally pick a keyword, because they show up in **orange**.)

Variables don't have to contain numbers. Find out how to use variables with letters and symbols on the next page.

VARIABLE

BANANAS

PUT YOUR BANANAS INTO ACTION

To use your 'bananas' variable actually to *do* something, you'll need to write some more code.

1. Imagine a monkey gets hungry and eats two bananas. To create another variable for the amount eaten, press return and type this:

```
>>> bananasEaten = 2
```

2. Press return to get to the next line, then type this formula to work out how many bananas the monkey has left:

```
>>> bananas - bananasEaten
```

3. Press return to get the answer. You should see this:

```
3
```

4. If the monkey finds more bananas, you can assign a new value to the 'bananas' variable. Press return and type a new value, such as 10:

```
>>> bananas = 10
```

5. Press return, retype the formula from step 2 and press return again. You'll get a different result, because the 'bananas' variable had a different value.

A STRING IS A THING YOU'LL USE A LOT

In Python, a word – or any collection of letters and symbols – is called a **string**. Strings are written inside quote marks. Here's how you put a string into a variable:

```
>>> exampleString = "I am a string."
```

String text inside quotation marks automatically shows up green.

Nom, nom, nom.

If you want to check the meaning of any Python or computing words, you can look at the glossary on pages 92-95.

STRING

LET THE USER DECIDE

If you want the user of a progam to decide what value a variable should have, you can use a **function** called `input()`.

In coding, any information entered by a user is known as 'input' (see blue box), but `input()` is a function that tells the computer to stop the program until the user has typed something and pressed return.

INPUT IN ACTION

You can use the `input()` function to ask for someone's name.

1. Open the Shell window and type:

```
>>> name = input("What is your name?")
```

This creates a variable called 'name'.

This tells the computer to run the **input** function AND stands for whatever the user types in.

2. Press return. The computer should now ask:

```
What is your name?
```

3. Type in your name next to the question and press return. Your name is now stored inside the variable, 'name'.

4. On the next line, type this:

```
>>> print(name)
```

Type the variable, 'name', not your own name here.

5. Press return. The computer should show your name in blue text on the next line.

INPUT AND OUTPUT

Anything you tell a computer, whether by typing, moving a mouse or loading a disk, counts as **input**. (That's not to be confused with the function **input()** in Python, which asks for input from a user.) Anything the computer sends back, whether shown on screen, printed out or burned onto a disk, is known as **output**.

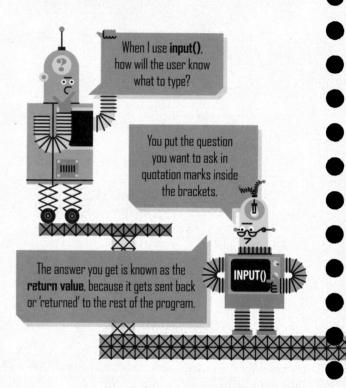

When I use **input()**, how will the user know what to type?

You put the question you want to ask in quotation marks inside the brackets.

The answer you get is known as the **return value**, because it gets sent back or 'returned' to the rest of the program.

INPUT()

DEBUGGING

If you get an error message, check you've copied the code exactly. Things to watch out for include:
- Have you used quote marks that match? So, **""** at both ends, not **"** at one end and **'** at the other.
- Have you missed any brackets?
- Is all your spelling correct?
- Have you got the right capital and lower case letters?

CREATE A CHARACTER

You can use **variables** and the **print()** and **input()** functions to create a character.

1. Open the Shell window. Click on **File** and select 'New File' – which brings up the Code window. Now click on **File** in the Code window, select 'Save As' and type in a name for your program.

2. Create a title to introduce your program by typing this:

```
print("Create your character!")
```

> This string will display on screen when the program runs.

3. Use the **input()** function to ask the user to decide the character's name.

```
name = input("What is your character called?")
```

4. Then, do the same for the character's age, strengths and weaknesses, each on a new line.

```
age = input("How old is your character?")
strengths = input("What are your character's strengths?")
weaknesses = input("What are your character's weaknesses?")
```

> Certain types of code automatically appear in certain colours. Variables are **black**, functions are **purple** and strings are **green**.

5. Now make the computer create the finished character using the **print()** function. (Put each instruction on a new line.)

```
print("Your character's name is", name)
print("Your character is", age, "years old")
print("Strengths:", strengths)
print("Weaknesses:", weaknesses)
print(name, "says, 'Thanks for creating me!'")
```

> **name** means the variable you created in step 3.

P.T.O. to see your code in action...

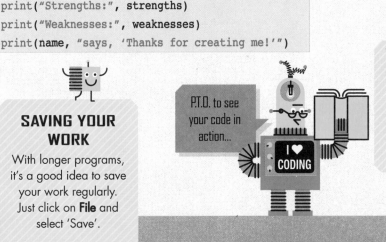

SAVING YOUR WORK

With longer programs, it's a good idea to save your work regularly. Just click on **File** and select 'Save'.

SPELLING STRINGS

Unlike the rest of your code, spelling doesn't matter inside strings. In fact, you can type any old nonsense, because the quotation marks tell the computer not to try to do anything with it.

6. Your program is finished. Click on **File** and select 'Save' to save it. Then click on the **Run** menu and select 'Run Module' from the drop-down list. The Shell window will open (or pop up in front of the Code window) and your text will appear in it.

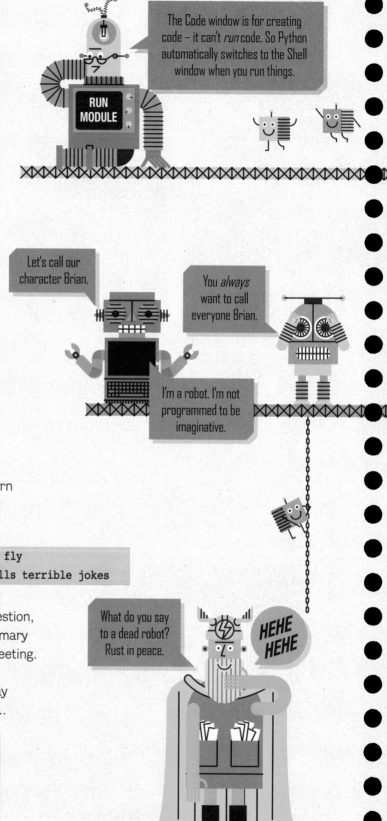

The Code window is for creating code – it can't *run* code. So Python automatically switches to the Shell window when you run things.

RUN MODULE

7. Try creating your own character by answering the questions that appear on screen. First, you'll see this:

```
Create your character!
What is your character called?
```

Output text appears in **blue**.

Let's call our character Brian.

You *always* want to call everyone Brian.

I'm a robot. I'm not programmed to be imaginative.

8. Fill in your character's name, then press return. On the next line, you should see:

```
How old is your character?
```

9. Fill in your character's age and press return again. Answer the following questions in the same way.

```
What are your character's strengths? Can fly
What are your character's weaknesses? Tells terrible jokes
```

10. When you press return after the final question, the code from step 5 runs, displaying a summary of your character on screen, along with a greeting.

It should look a bit like this (although you may have given your character different details)...

```
Your character's name is Brian
Your character is 245 years old
Strengths: Can fly
Weaknesses: Tells terrible jokes
Brian says, 'Thanks for creating me!'
```

What do you say to a dead robot? Rust in peace.

HEHE HEHE

ADDING NUMBERS AND STRINGS

When a user gives a program input, Python automatically stores it as a **string**. If the input is meant to be a *number*, you'll need to tell the computer to turn that string into a number.

Try this simple program, which displays how old you will be on your next birthday.

1. Start a new program and save it, as before. Then type this in the Code window:

```
age = input("How old are you?")
```

2. Create a new **variable** for how old you will be next birthday, and display it on screen.

```
ageNextYear = age + 1
print("You will be", ageNextYear, "next birthday.")
```

3. Try running that. You should get an error message when you press return. That's because the computer can't do the sum without turning the **input** into a number.

4. To fix this, you need to insert an extra function:

```
age = input("How old are you?")
ageNextYear = int(age) + 1
print("You will be", ageNextYear, "next birthday.")
```

> **int()** tells the computer to treat the variable inside the brackets as an 'integer' or whole number.

Save and run your code again. It should now work fine.

> Remember, a **string** is a word or set of symbols inside quotation marks – like the questions and answers in your create-a-character program.

RESTART

If you run the program more than once without closing the Shell window, the word **RESTART** will appear. This means the computer is no longer paying attention to anything above it. It's as though you've opened a fresh window.

INTEGER

FLOAT

INTEGERS AND FLOATS

There are two types of number in coding: *integers* and *floats*.

An **integer** is *always* a whole number, such as 2.

A **float** can be *any* number, including numbers with a decimal point, such as 2.5 – you can think of the decimal point 'floating' between the digits.

MAKING DECISIONS

To write a program that allows you to make decisions, the computer needs to react differently to different answers. For this, you need **conditions** to compare pieces of information, and **conditionals** to create different paths through the program.

WHAT ARE CONDITIONS?

A **condition** is a bit of code that compares two pieces of information. Conditions use **operators** (see page 9) to make these comparisons. For example, the operator == checks if two pieces of information are the same.

Open the Shell window and type this:

```
>>> age = 10
>>> age == 12
```

This creates a variable and sets its value to 10.

The == checks if the information on either side of it is equal.

Press return. You should see this on the next line:

```
False
```

The condition is False because 'age' is set to 10, not 12. To a computer, a condition can only *ever* be 'True' or 'False'. Try typing this into the Shell window, then press return:

```
>>> age = 10
>>> age == 10
```

This time, you should see 'True' on the next line.

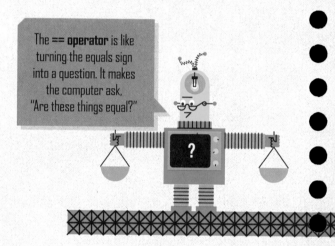

The == **operator** is like turning the equals sign into a question. It makes the computer ask, "Are these things equal?"

COMPARATIVE OPERATORS

These are symbols that the computer uses to *compare* two pieces of information. These will come in handy for some of the projects later in this book.

$==$ is equal to
$!=$ is not equal to
$<$ is less than
$>$ is greater than
$<=$ is less than or equal to
$>=$ is greater than or equal to

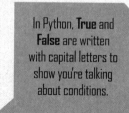

In Python, **True** and **False** are written with capital letters to show you're talking about conditions.

BOOLEANS

Another word for a **condition** is a **Boolean expression**. The true or false status of a Boolean expression is known as its **Boolean value.** You might come across these terms (named after a mathematician called George Boole) if you read about computing elsewhere.

WHAT ARE CONDITIONALS?

To use a **condition** in your code, you need a command called a **conditional**. Conditionals use conditions to test if something is **True** or **False**. Then they take a different path through the program, depending on the answer.

These paths are also known as **branches**, because of the tree-like structure they create.

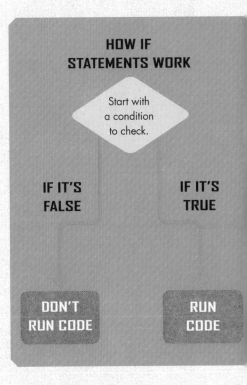

IF

One important **conditional** is known as an **if statement**, which tests whether a condition is True. *If* it is, the computer will follow the instruction after the **if statement**. If not, the computer will skip it. In Python, **if** is a keyword. Don't use it as a variable name, because the computer will think it's part of an **if statement** and get confused.

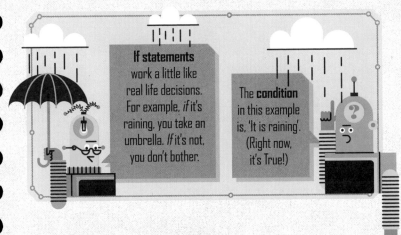

If statements work a little like real life decisions. For example, *if* it's raining, you take an umbrella. *If* it's not, you don't bother.

The **condition** in this example is, 'It is raining'. (Right now, it's True!)

HOW IF STATEMENTS WORK

Start with a condition to check.

IF IT'S FALSE	IF IT'S TRUE
DON'T RUN CODE	RUN CODE

Here's a program showing an **if statement** in action...

DO YOU LIKE ROBOTS?

1. Open a new file, and save it. Then type this line of code:

```
user_reply = input("Do you like robots? (Type yes or no)")
```

2. Press return and type this line:

```
if user_reply == "yes":
```

Use == to check if the user replies yes.

Conditionals and other **keywords** show up in orange.

Turn the page for the rest of the program.

3. Press return. The Code window should automatically add an **indent** of four spaces at the start of the next line. Type this after the indent:

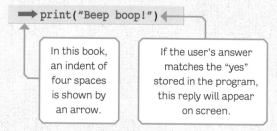

```
print("Beep boop!")
```

In this book, an indent of four spaces is shown by an arrow.

If the user's answer matches the "yes" stored in the program, this reply will appear on screen.

4. Save and run the program. If you type in 'yes', when asked if you like robots, the computer will print a cheerful 'Beep boop!' in reply.

If you type in 'no' (or anything else, for that matter), the program won't respond.

An **if statement** can include more branches if you include the keywords **else** and **elif**.

ELSE
The word '**else**' tells the computer which path to follow when the **condition** for **if** isn't met.

1. Open the program from the previous page and add these two lines below the final line:

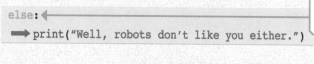

```
else:
    print("Well, robots don't like you either.")
```

Use the backspace key to delete the indent, so 'else' lines up with the 'if' above.

The completed code should look like this:

```
user_reply = input("Do you like robots? (Type yes or no)")
if user_reply == "yes":
    print("Beep boop!")
else:
    print("Well, robots don't like you either.")
```

Save and run the program. Try answering 'no' to activate the **else** part of the code.

INDENTS
Python uses blank spaces known as **indents** to group lines of code together, so the computer knows what to do next. Lines with the *same* indent run as a block, from top to bottom. Where a line is indented, it means it belongs to the line above it.

In this book, indents are shown like this:

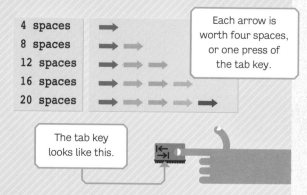

4 spaces	
8 spaces	
12 spaces	
16 spaces	
20 spaces	

Each arrow is worth four spaces, or one press of the tab key.

The tab key looks like this.

What if I want the computer to say something to people who don't like robots?

To do that, you'll need another type of conditional, called an **else** statement.

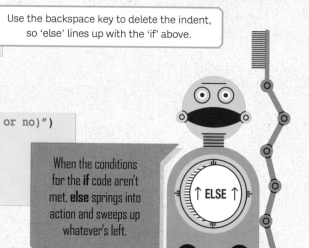

When the conditions for the **if** code aren't met, **else** springs into action and sweeps up whatever's left.

↑ ELSE ↑

ELIF

elif is short for 'else-if'. elif always comes after an **if** and springs into action when conditions for the **if** have not been met. It also has its own condition and only runs if *that* has been met.

An **else** isn't very specific. It's like replying 'none of the above' to a multiple-choice question.

elif allows your program to have more branching paths, and for each of those paths to unfold when the user gives a specific answer.

IF, ELIF AND ELSE

You could picture **if**, **elif** and **else** as a conveyor belt staffed by robots. **If** gets first pick, then **elif**. Finally, **else** sweeps up anything left over.

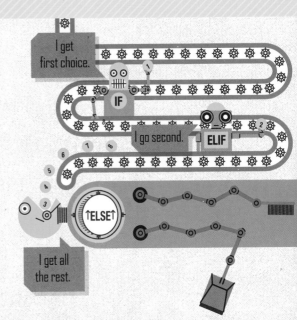

I get first choice.

I go second.

I get all the rest.

1. Save your robot program with a new name. Then type in the changes highlighted below:

```python
user_reply = input("Do you like robots? (Type yes, no, maybe or only ones with laser eyes)")
if user_reply == "yes":
    print("Beep boop!")
elif user_reply == "maybe":
    print("Make up your mind, human.")
elif user_reply == "only ones with laser eyes":
    print("Zzzap!")
elif user_reply == "no":
    print("Well, robots don't like you either.")
else:
    print("Your human nonsense offends us.")
```

2. Save and run the program. Try running it several times, choosing a different option each time. If you get an error message, check all the spelling and punctuation is correct, including in your answers. (See page 88-89 for more debugging tips.)

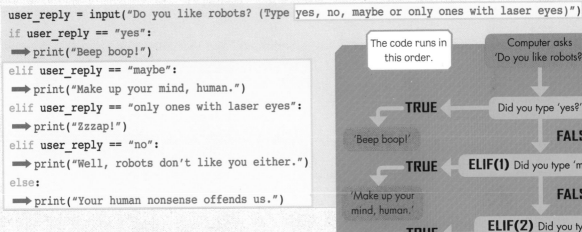

The code runs in this order.

Computer asks 'Do you like robots?'

Did you type 'yes?'

TRUE → 'Beep boop!'

FALSE

ELIF(1) Did you type 'maybe'?

TRUE → 'Make up your mind, human.'

FALSE

ELIF(2) Did you type 'only ones with laser eyes'?

TRUE → 'Zzzap!'

FALSE

ELIF(3) Did you type 'no'?

TRUE → Displays 'Well, robots don't like you either.'

FALSE

ELSE This option covers everything else.

Displays 'Your human nonsense offends us.'

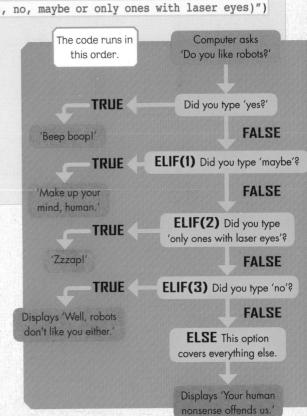

19

PLANNING PROGRAMS

When you're writing code with lots of branches, it's worth planning out what will happen on each branch. This helps you keep track of what's going on, so you end up with fewer errors in your code.

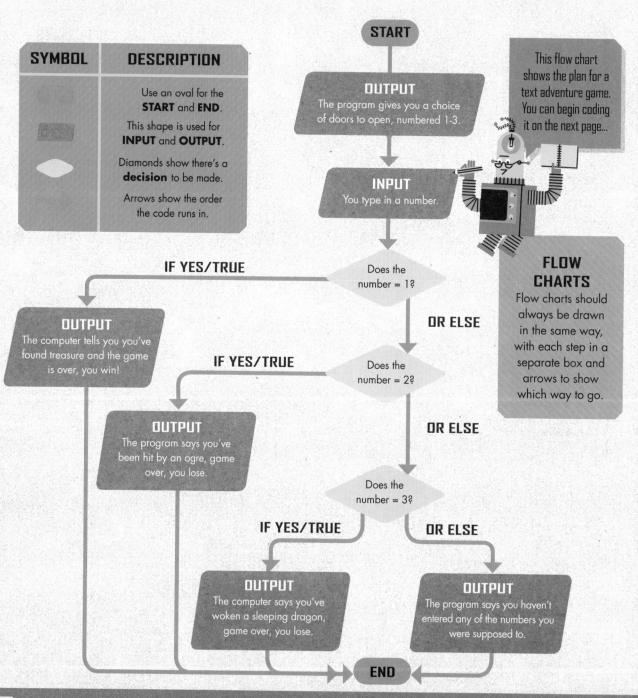

SYMBOL	DESCRIPTION
	Use an oval for the **START** and **END**.
	This shape is used for **INPUT** and **OUTPUT**.
	Diamonds show there's a **decision** to be made.
	Arrows show the order the code runs in.

START

OUTPUT
The program gives you a choice of doors to open, numbered 1-3.

INPUT
You type in a number.

This flow chart shows the plan for a text adventure game. You can begin coding it on the next page...

Does the number = 1?

IF YES/TRUE

OUTPUT
The computer tells you you've found treasure and the game is over, you win!

OR ELSE

Does the number = 2?

IF YES/TRUE

OUTPUT
The program says you've been hit by an ogre, game over, you lose.

OR ELSE

FLOW CHARTS
Flow charts should always be drawn in the same way, with each step in a separate box and arrows to show which way to go.

Does the number = 3?

IF YES/TRUE

OUTPUT
The computer says you've woken a sleeping dragon, game over, you lose.

OR ELSE

OUTPUT
The program says you haven't entered any of the numbers you were supposed to.

END

DARE YOU ENTER CASTLE DRAGONSNAX?

Now to make the game real...

1. Open a new file and save it, then set the scene using **print()**.

```
print("You are in a dark room in a mysterious castle.")
```

2. Press return. Now, give the player a choice between three mysterious doors.

```
print("In front of you are three doors. You must choose one.")
playerChoice = input("Choose 1, 2 or 3...")
```

3. Press return, then create an **if statement** using an == operator (see page 16) to test whether the player has chosen door 1.

```
if playerChoice == "1":
```

> Don't forget the colon.

4. Press return. Next, use **print()** to tell the program what to do if this happens.

> The indent means these lines will only run if the line before tells them to.

```
➡ print("You find a room full of treasure. You're rich!")
➡ print("GAME OVER, YOU WIN!")
```

5. Then, tell the program what to do if the user chooses the second door.

```
elif playerChoice == "2":
➡ print("The door opens and an angry ogre hits you with his club.")
➡ print("GAME OVER. YOU LOSE!")
```

6. Press return. Then, type the code that will run if the user chooses the third door:

```
elif playerChoice == "3":
➡ print("You go into the room and find a sleeping dragon.")
➡ print("The dragon wakes up and eats you. You are delicious.")
➡ print("GAME OVER. YOU LOSE!")
```

Press return.

Can I come out now?

Not until the code's finished.

...and that's why they call it Castle Dragonsnax.

BURP!

PLEASE TURN OVER TO CONTINUE

7. The user might type something other than 1, 2 or 3. To cover that, add an **else**.

```
else:
➡ print("Sorry, you didn't enter 1, 2 or 3!")
```

8. Finally, add a line that tells the user what to do when the game's over.

```
print("Run the game again to have another go.")
```

9. Save and run the program. Test it by running it several times, choosing a number from 1-3 each time. Then try typing something else, to test the **else** code.

When you're writing a program, you need to think through all the things a player might do. Unlike computers, humans don't always obey instructions...

HUMANS ARE NAUGHTY

Turn to page 87 for more about saving and running programs.

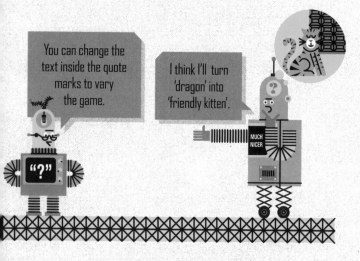

You can change the text inside the quote marks to vary the game.

I think I'll turn 'dragon' into 'friendly kitten'.

MUCH NICER

"?"

DEBUGGING

If you get an error message, check:
- Spelling
- Are there missing quote marks or brackets?
- Are all the **indents** correct?
- Have you accidentally used **=** instead of **==** in the **if** statements?
- Have you used **:** after **if**, **elif** and **else**?

RETURN TO CASTLE DRAGONSNAX

You can add more **if**, **elif** and **else** options to give the game more twists and turns. You can also add an element of chance, using a function called **randint()**.

1. Open your game and select 'Save As' in the File menu, then give it a different name. This saves a new version, so you can tinker with it without spoiling the original.

You can have as many number options as you like, as long as you add code to go with each one later.

EVERY OPTION NEEDS ITS OWN CODE.

2. The first few lines remain the same, except for slight changes to these lines, to create four door options:

```
print("In front of you are four doors. You must choose one.")
playerChoice = input("Choose 1, 2, 3 or 4...")
```

Only the highlighted text has changed.

3. Find the **print()** function about the sleeping dragon and delete the two lines which come *after* it.

```
elif playerChoice == "3":
    print("You go into the room and find a sleeping dragon.")
```

Delete the next two lines *after* this **print()** function.

4. Add three new **print** commands underneath, each on a new line:

```
    print("You can either:")
    print("1) Try to steal some of the dragon's gold.")
    print("2) Try to sneak around the dragon to the exit.")
```

These lines should all be indented four spaces. If this doesn't happen automatically, press tab or hit the space bar four times.

5. Press return. Now create a new variable, which allows the user to choose between stealing the dragon's gold or sneaking around it.

```
    dragonChoice = input("Type 1 or 2...")
```

These lines should line up with the **print()** functions in step 4.

6. Press return. Next, you need to create a new **if statement** which will run if the user chooses option 1 (steal the dragon's gold).

```
    if dragonChoice == "1":
```

7. On the next line, retype these lines from your original game.

```
        print("The dragon wakes up and eats you. You are delicious.")
        print("GAME OVER, YOU LOSE.")
```

These lines should automatically indent by eight spaces.

ROAR

FOR MORE VARIATIONS, TURN THE PAGE...

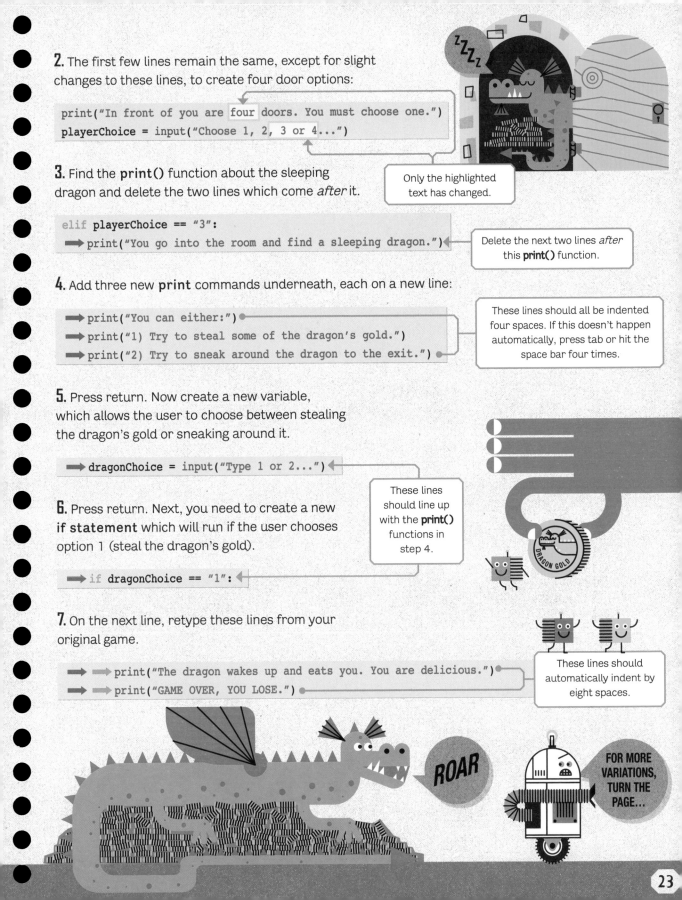

23

8. Press return. Now add an **elif** and two **print()** functions, like this, to create a branch that runs if the player chooses to sneak around the dragon.

YIPPEE!

ESCAPE!

```
elif dragonChoice == "2":
    print("You sneak around the dragon and escape the castle, blinking in the sunshine.")
    print("GAME OVER! YOU WIN!")
```

9. On the next line, add an **else**, which will run if the user doesn't type in 1 or 2.

```
else:
    print("Sorry, you didn't enter 1 or 2!")
```

Here's what your code so far should look like:

```
print("You are in a dark room in a mysterious castle.")
print("In front of you are four doors. You must choose one.")
playerChoice = input("Choose 1, 2, 3 or 4...")
if playerChoice == "1":
    print("You find a room full of treasure. You're rich!")
    print("GAME OVER, YOU WIN.")
elif playerChoice == "2":
    print("The door opens and an angry ogre hits you with his club.")
    print("GAME OVER, YOU LOSE.")
elif playerChoice == "3":
    print("You go into the room and find a sleeping dragon.")
    print("You can either:")
    print("1) Try to steal some of the dragon's gold.")
    print("2) Try to sneak around the dragon to the exit.")
    dragonChoice = input("Type 1 or 2...")
    if dragonChoice == "1":
        print("The dragon wakes up and eats you. You are delicious.")
        print("GAME OVER, YOU LOSE.")
    elif dragonChoice == "2":
        print("You sneak around the dragon and escape the castle, blinking in the sunshine.")
        print("GAME OVER! YOU WIN!")
    else:
        print("Sorry, you didn't enter 1 or 2!")
else:
    print("Sorry, you didn't enter 1, 2 or 3!")
print("Run the game again to have another go.")
```

This is the new section of code.

THE RANDOM SPHINX

10. After the code you added in step 9, create a new block of code, starting with an **elif**, to bring a sphinx into the game, and ask the user to guess a number:

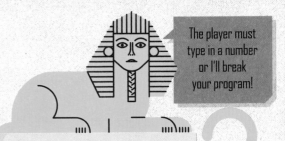

The player must type in a number or I'll break your program!

```
elif playerChoice == "4":
    print("You enter a room with a sphinx.")
    print("It asks you to guess what number it is thinking of, between 1 and 10.")
    number = int(input("What number do you choose?"))
```

You need **int()** to make sure the computer treats the answer as an integer (whole number).

11. To generate a random number for the sphinx, you need a new function, called **randint()**. All the random number functions are stored separately in something called a **module**. To access them, you need a **keyword** called **import**. Go to the very top of your program and type this:

```
import random
```

This loads the **random module** into your program.

IMPORTING FUNCTIONS

Some functions, like **print()**, can be put to work just by typing in the function name and brackets. These are called 'built-in' functions.

Other functions, like **randint()**, are stored in **modules** which need to be brought out of storage or **loaded** before you can use them. This is done using the command, **import**.

12. After the code you added in step 10, add an **if** with an **else** to create two branches in the program.

randint() generates a random number from 1-10.

```
if number == random.randint(1,10):
    print("The sphinx hisses in disappointment. You guessed correctly.")
    print("She must let you go free.")
    print("GAME OVER. YOU WIN!")
else:
    print("The sphinx tells you that your guess is incorrect.")
    print("You are now her prisoner forever.")
    print("GAME OVER, YOU LOSE.")
```

The **if** code runs *if* the player guesses correctly.

The **else** code runs if the player guesses incorrectly.

PLEASE TURN OVER TO CONTINUE

13. To complete the game, edit the final **else**. This code will run if the user doesn't type in a number between 1 and 4 at the beginning of the game. You'll need to edit the end of the string, like this:

```
else:
    print("Sorry, you didn't enter 1, 2, 3 or 4!")
```

Save and run the code to play the game. (Your last line should still be a **print()** function telling the user to run the game again to have another go.)

ADDING LOOPS

A **loop** just means a bit of code which repeats. Loops save you time, because you don't have to keep typing the same things over and over.

You can make your Castle Dragonsnax program restart automatically (without having to run it again) by adding a **while loop**.

WHILE LOOPS

A **while loop** repeats as long as a certain **condition** is true. In this program, that condition is 'the player has not typed EXIT at the end of the game'.

START

Main code runs until you win/lose.

Type **EXIT** or press **RETURN**

NO   Did you type **EXIT?**   YES

END

The flow chart above shows how the **while loop** works in this game.

Here, the loop means you can keep on playing without leaving the program.

DRAGONSNAX: THE LOOPY VERSION

1. Open the latest version of your game and save it with a new name. Go to the end of the first line:

```
import random
```

Press return to insert a new second line.

2. Create a variable, which will be used to set the **condition** for the **while loop**.

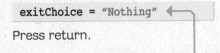
```
exitChoice = "Nothing"
```

Press return.

> The contents of the variable will be changed later, so it doesn't matter what you type inside the quotation marks.

3. On the next line, add a **while** command to start the **while loop**, like this:

```
while exitChoice != "EXIT":
```

> **!=** is the symbol for "does not equal".

This means that, unless the player types 'EXIT' at the end of the game, the program will keep running.

4. Go through and add an extra indent to *all* the rest of the code, so it is inside the **while loop**.

5. Replace the final print function (the one telling the user to run the game again) with this line:

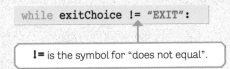
```
exitChoice = input("Press return to play again, or type EXIT to leave.")
```

This means the program will start the game again from the beginning if you press return, or stop running if you type 'EXIT'.

6. Save the program and run it several times. Pick a different path each time, to test all the branches.

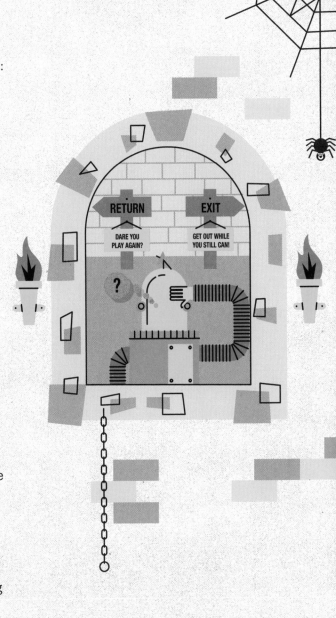

RETURN — DARE YOU PLAY AGAIN?

EXIT — GET OUT WHILE YOU STILL CAN!

?

CHAMPION CODER

THEY'RE HEEEERE!

Aliens are invading the Earth. This program gives humanity a chance to stop them. But the odds aren't on our side... these aliens multiply very, very quickly.

GLOBAL DEFENCE PROGRAM

You'll be creating a global defence network. This asks the player to guess the password for Earth's weapons – before it's too late.

1. Open a new file and save it, then create an 'aliens' variable, saying how many aliens have invaded in the first wave:

```
aliens = 2
```

2. Press return then create another variable.

```
password = "ALIENS"
```

EXPONENTS

To make the aliens in your program multiply rapidly, you'll need to use something called an **exponent** (also known as a **power**).

In maths, an exponent is written like this:
2^2 (means 2x2)
2^3 (means 2x2x2)
2^4 (means 2x2x2x2)
...and so on.
In Python, you use the operator ** to create an exponent.

3. Press return. Then tell the computer what to show on screen at the start.

```
print("Quickly! Aliens are invading the planet.")
print("You need to activate the global defence platforms.")
print("Hope you know the password, for Earth's sake...")
print()
print("--------------------------------------------------")
print("          WELCOME TO THE GLOBAL DEFENCE NETWORK          ")
print("--------------------------------------------------")
print()
```

> This will add a blank line.

> Use hyphens to create these dotted lines.

4. Press return and type this:

```
guess = input("Please enter the password: ").upper()
```

> This turns whatever you type into capital (or *upper* case) letters.

Don't bother taking me to your leader. We're here to destroy you all!

5. Press return and create a **while loop**. The loop will run as long as whatever you type in *does not* match the password stored in the program.

```
while guess != password:
```

!= means "does not equal".

6. Press return and add some **print** commands:

```
print()
print("INCORRECT PASSWORD.")
print()
```

This will show on screen if the password is guessed incorrectly.

7. Press return. Start the aliens multiplying, using the **exponent operator**, **. Then display the number of aliens with a **print** function.

```
aliens = aliens ** 2
print("There are", aliens, "aliens now on Earth. Try again!")
```

8. The next lines use an **if statement** with **break** (see yellow box) to stop the **while loop** *if* the aliens outnumber humans, ending the game.

```
if aliens > 7400000000:
    break
```

The game assumes there are 7.4 billion humans.

9. The following lines will run as long as the aliens do *not* outnumber humans.

```
print()
print("Password hint: the things that are attacking us.")
print()
guess = input("Quick! Please enter the password: ").upper()
```

10. Finish with an **if/else statement**, like this. The **if** code will run *if* the aliens go over 7.4 billion. The **else** code will run if you guess the password correctly.

```
if aliens > 7400000000:
    print("Nooooooo! The aliens have outnumbered us. All is lost.")
else:
    print("Hooray! We won the fight and the world is saved!")
```

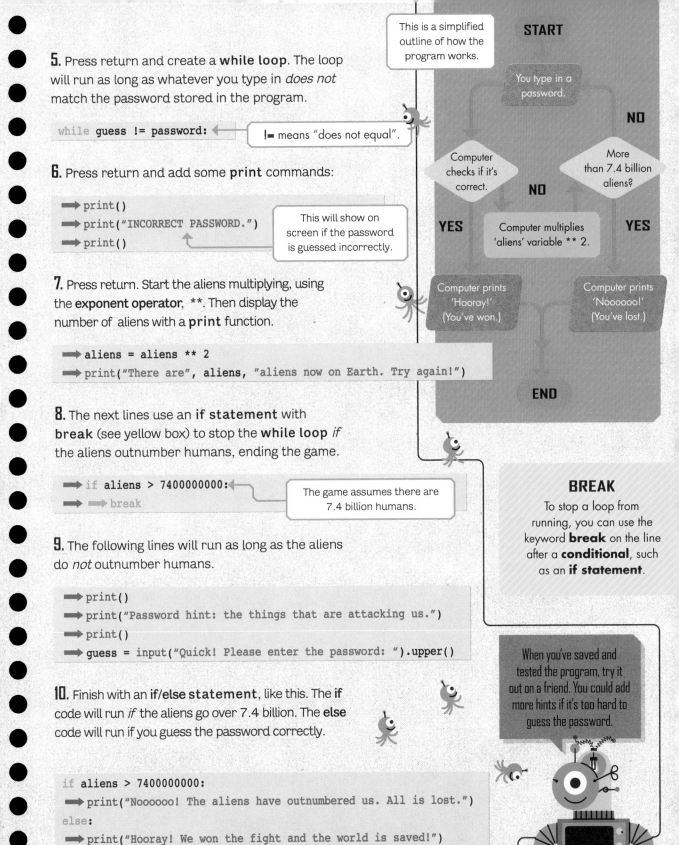

This is a simplified outline of how the program works.

START

You type in a password.

Computer checks if it's correct.

NO

More than 7.4 billion aliens?

NO

YES

Computer multiplies 'aliens' variable ** 2.

YES

Computer prints 'Hooray!' (You've won.)

Computer prints 'Noooooo!' (You've lost.)

END

BREAK

To stop a loop from running, you can use the keyword **break** on the line after a **conditional**, such as an **if statement**.

When you've saved and tested the program, try it out on a friend. You could add more hints if it's too hard to guess the password.

GUESSING GAME

You can create a simple guessing game using **conditions**, **conditionals**, randomly-generated numbers and **loops** – that is, all stuff you know already.

In this game, the computer will generate a random number from 1-20, which you then try to guess.

1. Start by opening a new program and importing the **random module**. Then use **randint()** to generate the number.

```
import random
number = random.randint(1,20)
```

In Python, **modules** are files which store functions you don't need all the time. Modules are only loaded when you ask for them – keeping the main part of Python smaller and quicker to run.

2. Ask the player to guess a number, and store the answer as a variable, called 'guess'.

```
guess = int(input("I'm thinking of a number from 1 to 20. What is it?"))
```

Press return.

3. Now begin a **while loop**. (This will keep the game running until the player guesses correctly.)

```
while guess != number:
```

Remember **!=** means 'does not equal'.

CONVERTING THE INPUT

Python will automatically read anything the player types in as a **string**, unless you convert it into a whole number or 'integer' using the function **int()**.

4. Press return. On the next line, add an **if statement** that will check if the guess is *lower* than the number the computer has generated.

```
if guess < number:
```

< means 'less than'.

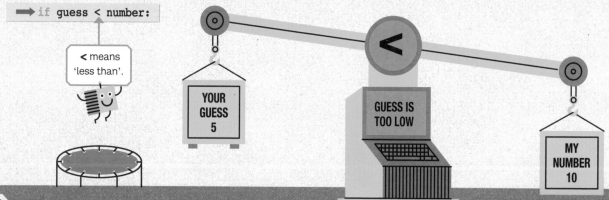

YOUR GUESS 5

GUESS IS TOO LOW

MY NUMBER 10

5. Press return. The next line should automatically have two indents. Type this:

```
print("Your number was too low...")
```

This message will appear if the player's guess is *lower* than the computer's number.

6. Press return and delete one indent. Now add an **else** and another **print()** function.

```
else:
    print("Your number was too high...")
```

This will appear if the guess is *higher* than the computer's number.

7. Press return, and ask the player to guess again. Since the **while loop** keeps the code running until the player guesses correctly, this text will appear every time the guess is wrong.

```
guess = int(input("Please try again..."))
```

8. Press return, delete the indent and add a final line. As it's not indented, it's outside the **while loop**.

```
print("Congratulations! Correct answer!")
```

This runs once the player has guessed correctly.

9. Save and run the program to test it. This is what the finished code will look like on screen.

```python
import random
number = random.randint(1,20)
guess = int(input("I'm thinking of a number from 1 to 20. What is it?"))
while guess != number:
    if guess < number:
        print("Your number was too low...")
    else:
        print("Your number was too high...")
    guess = int(input("Please try again..."))
print("Congratulations! Correct answer!")
```

Don't worry if you run into a few bugs. Fixing them is a good way to learn more about how code works.

Make sure you open and close both sets of brackets in steps 2 and 7. It's easy to cause a bug by missing one.

FOR LOOPS

A **while loop** makes a section of code repeat and repeat until a certain **condition** is met. If you want to say exactly *how many* times it should repeat, you can use a **for loop**.

WHILE LOOP

While loops only stop when something changes. If it doesn't change, they could go on forever.

This is a bit like playing musical chairs, where you keep moving until the music stops.

FOR LOOP

With **for loops**, you can tell them exactly *when* to stop.

LAP TIME
7.50.61

It's a bit like running laps around a sports field, where you run as many laps as you've been told.

HOW MANY TIMES?

Each time you use a **for loop**, you need to tell it how many times to repeat. To do this you need a type of **function** called **range()**.

To create a very simple **for loop** using **range()**, open a new file, save it, and type this:

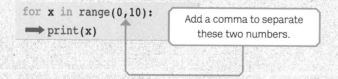

```
for x in range(0,10):
    print(x)
```

Add a comma to separate these two numbers.

RANGE()

When you use the **range()** function, it creates a list of numbers. The numbers you type inside the brackets tell the computer where the list starts and ends.

for x in range() tells the computer to run the following code *once for each entry* in the list.

WHAT DOES IT DO?

If you run the code you typed in on the previous page, you should see the numbers 0-9 appear in the Shell window.

0 1 2 3 4 5 6 7 8 9 10

Why does it count from 0-9 not 0-10, like the numbers in the brackets?

That's because the second number in the **range( )** brackets tells the computer to stop counting *before* that number.

THE NUTS AND BOLTS

This **for loop** has a lot going on, so here's a breakdown of the parts of the code and what they do.

for... in are keywords that tell the computer to go through the list that follows, in order, taking a different item from the list each time.

The letter 'x' here is a **variable**. (You could call it anything you like.)

```
for x in range(0,10):
    print(x)
```

The **print()** function tells the computer to display the 'x' variable on screen. Each time the **for loop** runs, the value of 'x' changes.

The **range()** function creates a list of numbers. This list controls how many times the loop will run.

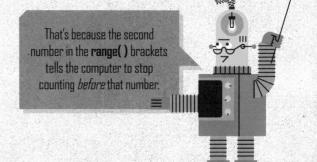

Part of what makes Python so powerful is because it packs a lot into not many words.

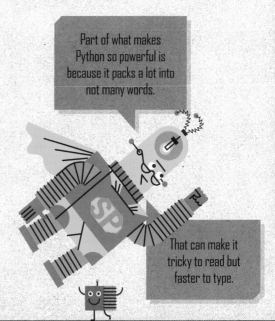

That can make it tricky to read but faster to type.

A TIMES TABLES SHORTCUT

You can use **for loops** to get Python work out the times tables for you. Here's how.

1. Open a new file, give it a name and type:

```
table = int(input("Please enter a times table: "))
```

This creates a **variable**, 'table', to stand for whatever number the user types in when the program runs. This will be the times table that gets printed at the end.

> Remember, **int()** turns a string into an integer (whole number), so whatever is typed in when the program runs is treated as a number.

2. Press return, then type this **for loop**, using the **range()** function:

```
for x in range(0,13):
```

> This **range** goes from 0 to 12.

3. Press return, then type this, to make the computer display the times table the user has asked for.

```
print (x, "x", table, "=", x*table)
```

> This is the 'multiply' **operator.**

> The text in quote marks will appear on screen.

> This program multiplies all the numbers from 0-12 by the number you enter at the start.

4. Save and run the program. You should see the times table you chose appear on screen, like this:

```
0 x 7 = 0
1 x 7 = 7
2 x 7 = 14
3 x 7 = 21
4 x 7 = 28
5 x 7 = 35
```

(And so on, up to 12 x 7.)

> Once you've run it successfully, try changing the values in **range()**. But don't make the second number *too* big, or it will take ages to run.

WAITING...
WAITING...
WAITING...

NESTED LOOPS

If you put one loop inside another, this is known as a **nested loop**.

Here's a program using **nested for loops** that prints out some robot sounds.

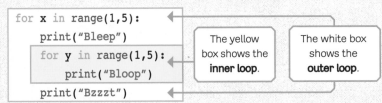

```
for x in range(1,5):
    print("Bleep")
    for y in range(1,5):
        print("Bloop")
    print("Bzzzt")
```

The yellow box shows the **inner loop**.

The white box shows the **outer loop**.

NESTED VS NOT

An ordinary, non-nested loop allows you to repeat a section of code without having to type it out again.

A **nested loop** allows you to repeat *two or more* sections of code, for an even bigger shortcut.

(The best coders are lazy coders: the less you have to type, the better.)

Here's how it works:

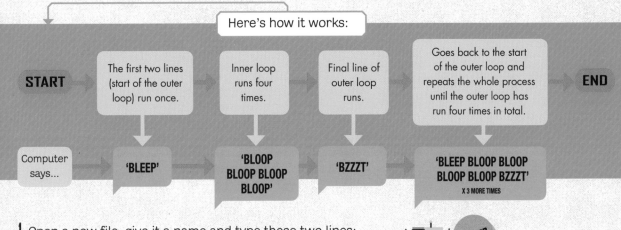

| START | The first two lines (start of the outer loop) run once. | Inner loop runs four times. | Final line of outer loop runs. | Goes back to the start of the outer loop and repeats the whole process until the outer loop has run four times in total. | END |

| Computer says... | 'BLEEP' | 'BLOOP BLOOP BLOOP BLOOP' | 'BZZZT' | 'BLEEP BLOOP BLOOP BLOOP BLOOP BZZZT' X 3 MORE TIMES |

1. Open a new file, give it a name and type these two lines:

```
for x in range(1,5):
    print("Bleep")
```

This makes the outer loop run 4 times.

2. Then create the inner loop:

```
    for y in range(1,5):
        print("Bloop")
```

The inner loop also runs 4 times.

Code inside the inner loop has a *double* indent.

3. On the next line, add another **print()** function to complete the outer loop. This should line up with the **print()** function from step 1.

```
    print("Bzzzt")
```

A single indent means you're back in the *outer* loop.

4. Save and run the program. You should see a repeating pattern of robot sounds.

The sounds should repeat in this pattern.

```
Bleep
Bloop
Bloop
Bloop
Bloop
Bzzzt
Bleep
Bloop
Bloop
Bloop
Bloop
Bzzzt
Bleep
Bloop
Bloop
Bloop
Bloop
Bzzzt
Bleep
Bloop
Bloop
Bloop
Bloop
Bzzzt
```

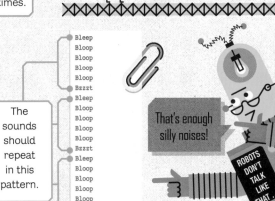

That's enough silly noises!

ROBOTS DON'T TALK LIKE THAT ...

35

USING LISTS

Python allows you to group lots of pieces of information together by making a **list**. Lists are stored using variables.

MAKING A LIST

You create a list using square brackets, like this:

```
spacelist = ["rocket", "planet", "asteroid", "alien"]
```

The items in the list are separated by commas.

If you want to do anything with one of the words from that list, you can use something called the **index** – the position of the item in the list.

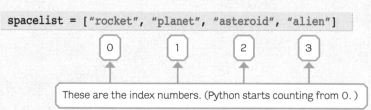

```
spacelist = ["rocket", "planet", "asteroid", "alien"]
        0        1          2           3
```

These are the index numbers. (Python starts counting from 0.)

Indexes aren't used only with lists. You can also have an index for the characters in a variable (see page 44).

There are lots of ways to dip into a list and do things with the items in it.

DISPLAYING ITEMS FROM A LIST

1. Open a new file and create your list:

```
spacelist = ["rocket", "planet", "asteroid", "alien"]
```

2. To display an item from the list, use **print()**.

```
print(spacelist[0])
```

Put the index number of the item you want in square brackets.

3. Save and run your program. If you followed the example above, you should see this:

```
rocket
```

SPACELIST

[0]

DISPLAYING THE WHOLE LIST

1. You can use a **for loop** to display the whole list. Delete the second line of your program and add this:

```
for item in spacelist:
    print(item)
```

'item' is a variable that stands for each item in the list.

2. Save and run the program now. You should see this:

```
rocket
planet
asteroid
alien
```

The **for loop** runs once for each item in the list, printing each item on a new line.

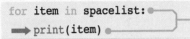

You can display the list by typing **print(spacelist)** but it won't look as nice.

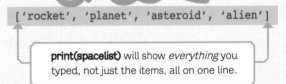

```
['rocket', 'planet', 'asteroid', 'alien']
```

print(spacelist) will show *everything* you typed, not just the items, all on one line.

REPLACING, DELETING, ADDING

1. You can replace an item by entering a new one. Try inserting this line before the **for loop**.

```
spacelist[0] = "planet zarg"
```

This replaces the first item ('rocket') with a new one ('planet zarg').

2. Save and run the program. The first item in the list should now be 'planet zarg'.

3. To *delete* an item, replace the line you just added:

```
del spacelist[0]
```

4. Save and run the program. The first item (at index '0') should now be 'planet' (as 'planet zarg' has been deleted).

5. You can *add* an item to the end of a list using **append**.

```
spacelist.append("moon")
```

If you run the program now, the last item will be 'moon'.

If you want to keep different versions of a program, just give it a new name each time you save it.

DEL AND APPEND

The command **del** deletes an item and reshuffles the index.

The command **append** adds an item to the end of the list.

ADDING LISTS TOGETHER

1. You can also add lists together. Open a new file and type:

```
spacelist1 = ["rocket", "planet", "asteroid", "alien"]
spacelist2 = ["space station", "star", "black hole"]
spacelist = spacelist1 + spacelist2
for item in spacelist:
    print(item)
```

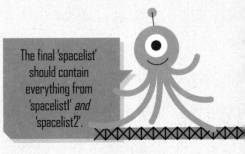

The final 'spacelist' should contain everything from 'spacelist1' *and* 'spacelist2'.

2. Save and run the program. You should see a list with all 7 items.

A GAME OF CONSEQUENCES

There's a party game called 'Consequences', where people make up stories by throwing together random characters, places and events, like this...

THE CONSEQUENCE WAS...

WOMAN'S NAME...

SHE SAID...

MAN'S NAME...

HE SAID...

WHERE THEY MET...

THE WORLD SAID...

THE CONSEQUENCE (WHAT HAPPENED) WAS...

Here's how to create a Python version of the game that makes up stories at random in an instant.

1. Open a new file, give it a name and save it. Then create a list, like this:

```
woman = ["A scientist", "A queen", "A pirate", "A giant rabbit"]
```

These are just suggestions. You could include any characters you like.

The program will pick one of these at random as the female character in your story.

2. Next, create a list of male characters:

```
man = ["a police officer", "an artist", "your grandfather", "a killer robot"]
```

3. Then, create lists for the other parts of your story, like this:

```
place = ["on Pluto.", "at the supermarket.", "in a spooky, bat-filled cave."]
sheWore = ["scuba diving gear.", "fairy wings.", "a paper bag."]
heWore = ["a purple suit.", "a shark costume.", "a beach towel."]
womanSays = ["'Who are you?'", "'How many beans make five?'", "'Why?'"]
manSays = ["'Beep boop!'", "'Don't eat frogs!'", "'What time do you call this?'"]
consequence = ["world peace.", "chaos.", "a giant foot squashed them.", "rainbows."]
worldSaid = ["'Errant nonsense!'", "'Cheese is trending now.'", "'I'm melting!'"]
```

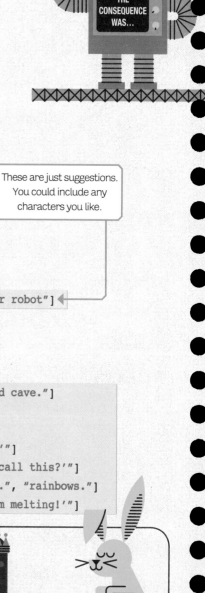

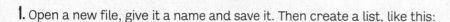

4. To turn your lists into a story, you'll need the **random module** (to pick things from the lists) and a **while loop** (to create a new story each time you press return).

RANDOM. CHOICE()

If you want to pick an item at random from a list you need the **random.choice()** function. (You specify which list inside the brackets.)

Import the **random module** and open a **while loop**, like this:

```
import random
while True:
```

Typing 'while True' at the start of a **while loop** makes the loop run forever (or until you close the program).

5. To start the story, you need to pick the characters and place, and put them into a sentence. Type the following (this should be indented):

```
print(random.choice(woman), "met", random.choice(man), random.choice(place))
```

This picks a random item from the list called 'woman'.

This adds the word 'met'.

This picks a random item from the 'man' list.

This picks a random item from the 'place' list.

6. Then do the same for the other lists, like this:

```
print("She was wearing", random.choice(sheWore))
print("He was wearing", random.choice(heWore))
print("She said,", random.choice(womanSays))
print("He said,", random.choice(manSays))
print("The consequence was", random.choice(consequence))
print("The world said,", random.choice(worldSaid))
```

7. End the program by printing a blank line, then ask the user to press return for another story. (You can close the window to stop the program.)

```
print()
input("Press enter to play again.")
print()
```

The **while loop** will pause until the user hits return.

'A queen met a killer robot on Pluto. She was wearing a paper bag...'

8. Save and run the program, and see what stories you get. If you like, you could play around with the lists to create even more versions.

DICTIONARIES

Like **lists**, **dictionaries** are a way of storing information in Python.
Each entry in a dictionary is paired with a label, called a **key**.
You look up entries using the keys.

CREATING A DICTIONARY

You set up a dictionary like a list, but with the items inside curly brackets. For example...

1. To make a dictionary that stores superhero names and powers, open the Shell window and type this:

> This is the name of the dictionary.

> The **key** goes *before* the entry. (Here, the keys are the names.)

> A colon links each key with its entry or **value**. (The values are the superpowers.)

```
>>> powers = {"The Pigeon": "flight", "Brainzar": "mind reader", "Cyborg": "controls machines"}
```

> Commas separate different items.

2. You can display an entry (or superpower) by typing in the key (the name). So if you type this:

```
>>> print (powers["The Pigeon"])
```

> This will display the value associated with this key.

You should see this:

```
flight
```

3. To add a new item to the dictionary, type this:

```
>>> powers["Laser Girl"] = "shoots lasers"
```

> Dictionaries don't list items in any particular order, so you might see the items in a different order each time.

4. You can also display the whole dictionary.

```
>>> print(powers)
```

> This will include Laser Girl.

If you do this now, you should see something like:

```
{'Cyborg': 'controls machines', 'Brainzar': 'mind reader', 'The Pigeon': 'flight',
'Laser Girl': 'shoots lasers'}
```

5. You can also delete items.

```
>>> del powers["The Pigeon"]
```

If you display the dictionary now, The Pigeon should be gone.

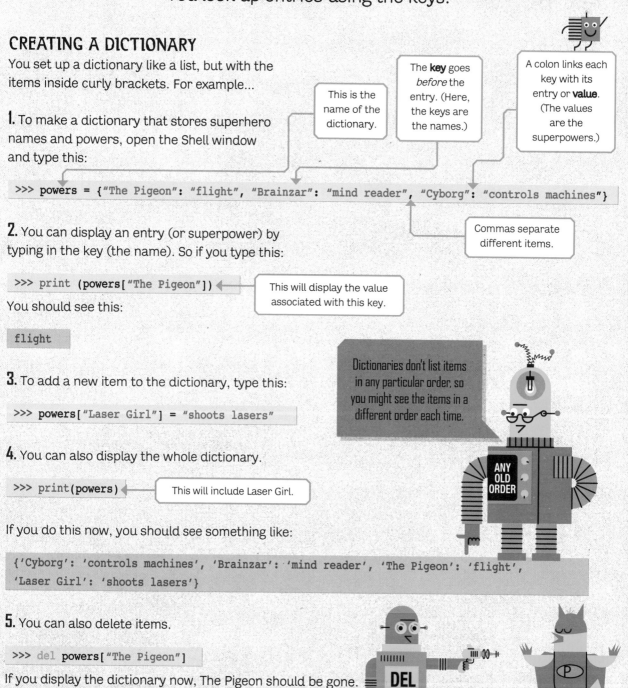

6. To change the **value** of a dictionary entry, try this:

```
>>> powers["Brainzar"] = "seeing the future"
```

If you display the dictionary now, Brainzar will have a new power.

ALIEN TRANSLATOR

You can use dictionaries to create a translation program for an alien language.

Hmm, how do you say, 'I welcome our new alien overlords...'?

HOW TO SPEAK ALIEN

1. Open and save a new program in the Code window. Then create your dictionary.

```
alienDictionary = {"we": "vorag", "come": "thang", "in": "zon",
"peace": "argh", "hello": "kodar", "can": "znak", "i": "az", "borrow": "liftit",
"some": "zum", "rocket": "upgoman", "fuel": "kakboom", "please": "selpin",
"don't": "baaaaaaaaaaaaarn", "shoot": "flabil", "welcome": "unkip",
"our": "mandig", "new": "brang", "alien": "marangin", "overlords": "bap"}
```

Type this all in lower case.

2. Now ask the user to enter something to translate:

```
englishPhrase = input("Please enter an English word or phrase to translate: ")
englishWords = englishPhrase.lower().split()
```

lower() turns whatever the user enters into lower case letters.

split() turns a string into a list of words by splitting it at the spaces.

3. Next, create a list, which will be used to print out the translated phrase, and a **for loop** to cycle through the dictionary, checking if the English words typed are there.

This creates a blank list.

This **for loop** will run as many times as there are words to translate.

```
alienWords = []
for word in englishWords:
    if word in alienDictionary:
        alienWords.append(alienDictionary[word])
    else:
        alienWords.append(word)
print("In alien, say: ", " ".join(alienWords))
```

If a typed word is in the **dictionary**, this looks up the **value** (alien word) for the **key** (English word) and adds it to the 'alienWords' list.

This adds words *not* in the dictionary to the 'alienWords' list, untranslated.

Type one space here.

This displays the translation in alien.

Save and run the program to try it out.

" ".join() joins all the words in the 'alienWords' list back into one string, adding one space in between.

HOW TO SPEAK ALIEN

SPY MESSAGES

Spies use a technique called encryption to scramble the letters in their messages, so no one can understand them without a secret formula to unscramble them again. You can use Python to create your own encryption program.

CAESAR CIPHER

A **Caesar Cipher** is an encryption method that takes the letters of the message you want to send and 'shifts' each letter along the alphabet a certain number of places. The number of places moved along is known as the shift amount, or 'key'.

For example, if the first letter of the word you want to encrypt is C, and the key is 6, the letter will become I.

Roman Emperor Julius Caesar is thought to have used this code to send secret orders to his soldiers.

The inner ring of this wheel shows the alphabet shifted along 6 places. Can you use it to decode what the robot spy is saying below?

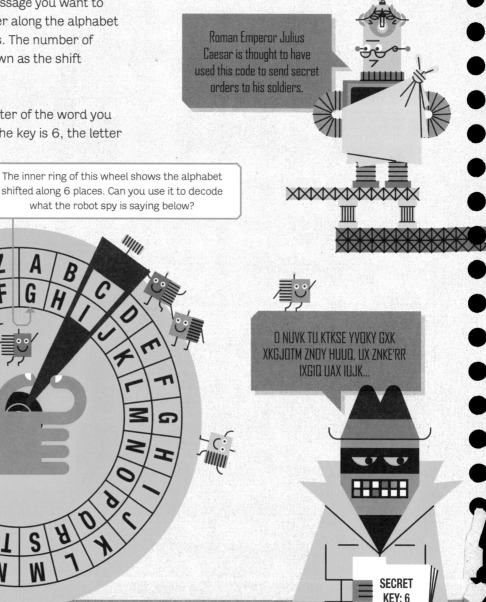

O NUVK TU KTKSE YVOKY GXK XKGJOTM ZNOY HUUQ, UX ZNKE'RR IXGIQ UAX IUJK...

SECRET KEY: 6

CREATING YOUR CIPHER

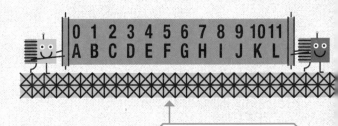

1. Open a new file and save it. On the first line, create a **variable** that contains a **string** with the whole alphabet, typed out twice.

```
alphabet = "ABCDEFGHIJKLMNOPQRSTUVWXYZABCDEFGHIJKLMNOPQRSTUVWXYZ"
```

Each character in a **string** has an **index**, just like each entry in a **list**.

First alphabet	Second alphabet

You need the second alphabet to give you somewhere to shift to once you get to Z.

For example, if your key is 10 and your letter is a Z, you need to shift fowards through A to J.

Having two alphabets allows you a key of up to 25. Well, technically 26, but that would shift you back to your original message, which wouldn't be very secret.

2. Next, ask the user to enter a message.

```
stringToEncrypt = input("Please enter a message to encrypt: ")
```

3. In case the message includes lower case letters, make the string all upper case with the function, **upper()**.

```
stringToEncrypt = stringToEncrypt.upper()
```

This turns any lower case letters into upper case, so they match the letters in your alphabet variable.

4. Next, ask the user to type in a number. This will be used as the key to encrypt their message.

```
shiftAmount = int(input("Please enter a whole number from 1-25 to be your key."))
```

5. Now, create a blank string. This is where the encrypted message will be stored when your program runs.

```
encryptedString = ""
```

> Typing a pair of empty quote marks, like this, creates a blank string.

6. To encrypt your message, you need to shift each letter in turn. You can do this with a **for loop**, using the **index** of each letter to work out what it will become.

> The **for loop** runs once for every letter in the message you're encrypting.

> The **find()** function searches the 'alphabet' variable for the first appearance of your 'currentCharacter', and sends back its **index**.

```
for currentCharacter in stringToEncrypt:
    position = alphabet.find(currentCharacter)
    newPosition = position + shiftAmount
    encryptedString = encryptedString + alphabet[newPosition]
```

> This adds the shift amount, or key, to the **index** you just found.

> This looks up the shifted letter and adds it to your encrypted message.

Here's what's happening in the code above. Imagine you've typed in the word 'dog' to encrypt, and a key of 2.

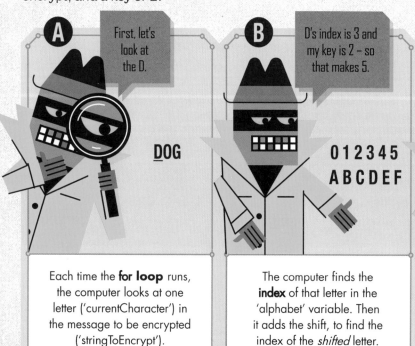

A First, let's look at the D.

DOG

Each time the **for loop** runs, the computer looks at one letter ('currentCharacter') in the message to be encrypted ('stringToEncrypt').

B D's index is 3 and my key is 2 – so that makes 5.

0 1 2 3 4 5
A B C D E F

The computer finds the **index** of that letter in the 'alphabet' variable. Then it adds the shift, to find the index of the *shifted* letter.

C The letter 'f' has an index of 5, so that's the first letter of the encrypted message.

D → F

The computer looks up the shifted letter and inserts it into a new string ('encryptedString'). Then it repeats the process, until it has encrypted all the letters.

7. The last line in your program is *not* indented. This means it will run when the **for loop** has finished.

```
print("Your encrypted message is", encryptedString)
```

This will show the user's encrypted message on the screen.

DEBUGGING TIPS
- Check your indents.
- Make sure you've used = and == in the correct places.
- Make sure your variable names are spelled the same way each time, with the same capital and lower case letters.

See pages 88-89 for more about debugging.

8. Save and run the program. Then test it by typing in a word and a key. For example, if you type 'dog' and '2', you should see this:

```
Your encrypted message is FQI
```

Your encrypted message will appear in capital letters.

ALL CAPS

ADDING PUNCTUATION

9. If you want your spy messages to include punctuation and symbols, you can add the lines highlighted below, so your **for loop** looks like this:

This line becomes indented below the **if statement**.

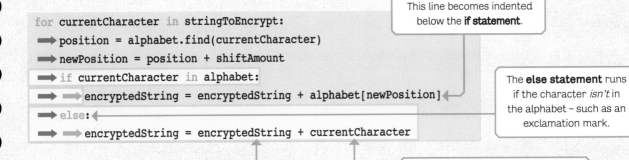

```
for currentCharacter in stringToEncrypt:
    position = alphabet.find(currentCharacter)
    newPosition = position + shiftAmount
    if currentCharacter in alphabet:
        encryptedString = encryptedString + alphabet[newPosition]
    else:
        encryptedString = encryptedString + currentCharacter
```

The **else statement** runs if the character *isn't* in the alphabet – such as an exclamation mark.

If the character isn't in the alphabet, it will just be added to the encrypted message as it is.

DECRYPTION

Spies also need to decode messages they receive. Unjumbling an encrypted message is known as *decryption*.

To decrypt messages you've encrypted using this program, you need a *decryption* key. This is a negative version of your shift. So, if your original shift was 2, your decryption key will be -2.

Try feeding your encrypted message through the program using this key. For example, if your encrypted message is 'FQI', type that in, with a new decryption key of -2 and you should get...

...ME!

TURTLE DRAWING

You can create images or **graphics** in Python using a **module** called **turtle** – a set of ready-made functions designed for drawing shapes and lines.

WHAT IS A TURTLE?

A turtle is like a cursor that moves around your screen, leaving a line behind it. Turtles can draw all kinds of shapes and pictures – you just need to give them the right commands.

> You can choose a few different styles for your turtle. This is one called, not very surprisingly, 'turtle'.

DRAWING A SQUARE

To use **turtle**, you first need to **import** the **turtle module**. This short program shows you how to import it and use it to draw a square.

1. Open a new file and save it. Then load the turtle module, like this:

```
from turtle import *
```

> **import *** imports all the turtle commands so you don't have to type 'turtle' in front of them each time you use one.

2. Set the colour the turtle will use to draw.

```
color("blue")
```

> Make sure you use the American spelling of 'color'.

3. On the next line, set the style of the turtle with a function called **shape**:

```
shape("turtle")
```

> You could swap in another style from the 'turtle styles' box.

TURTLE STYLES
Here are the other turtle styles.

arrow ◀
circle ●
square ■
triangle ◀
classic ◀

TURTLE COLOURS
Turtle doesn't have every colour in the world, but it has quite a few, including some with exotic names. You can try any of these:

aquamarine		goldenrod	
cyan		lemon chiffon	
plum		HotPink	
dark orchid		DarkKhaki	
LimeGreen		DarkOrange	

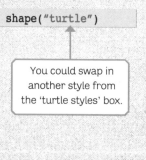

4. Set the turtle's speed, choosing a number between 1 and 10 (10 is the fastest).

```
speed(10)
```

5. You can set the thickness of the line your turtle will draw using a function called **pensize**.

```
pensize(4)
```
This gives you a fairly thick line. ━━━━━

FIRST TURTLES

The name 'turtle' comes from a type of robot that moves around the floor, drawing with a pen in its tail. The first programming language to use turtles was called LOGO.

6. Now, tell your turtle where to go...

```
forward(50)
right(90)
forward(50)
right(90)
forward(50)
right(90)
forward(50)
```
This moves the turtle forward 50 pixels (see right).

This turns the turtle clockwise by 90 degrees.

PIXELS

The distances turtles move are measured in **pixels** – the dots that make up the pictures on a computer screen.

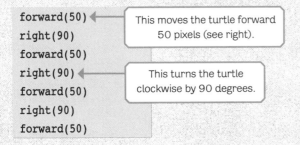

360°/0°
270°
90°
180°

There are 360 degrees in a full turn.

DIFFERENT SHAPES

You can change the code in step 6 to get different shapes:

Triangle	Octagon
	Use a **for loop** to draw a shape with eight sides:

7. Save and run your program.
You should see this:

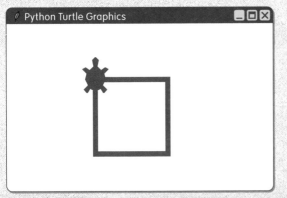

Python Turtle Graphics

```
Triangle

forward(50)
left(120)
forward(50)
left(120)
forward(50)
```

```
Octagon

for x in range(8):
    ➡ forward(50)
    ➡ right(45)
```

Or try making your own shapes by combining these functions and adding amounts inside the brackets:

```
forward()          left()

backward()         right()
```

DRAWING SNOWFLAKES WITH TURTLES

You can make your turtle draw a snowflake using **loops** and **functions** to build a repeating pattern.

Putting instructions inside a function means you can repeat them by just using the function, instead of having to type everything in again.

1. Open a new file and set up your turtle in the same way as before.

```
from turtle import *
shape("turtle")
speed(10)
pencolor("white")
pensize(6)
```

We chose white to make the drawing look snowy.

2. Make a coloured background by getting the turtle window and setting a colour for it. (We chose turquoise.)

```
Screen().bgcolor("turquoise")
```

Screen() is a function which gets the turtle window or 'screen'.

The function **bgcolor()** sets a background colour, and the **.** links it to your window.

HIDING THE TURTLE
If you don't want to see the turtle itself, you can use a function called **hideturtle**. Try adding this at the end of the code from step 1.

```
hideturtle()
```

Do you wanna build a snowman?

Nah, my hands would rust.

3. Now you're going to create a function called **vshape**, to draw the first bit of the snowflake in the shape of a 'v'.

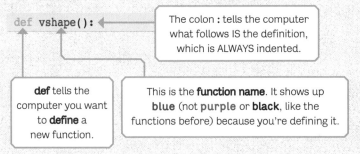

```
def vshape():
```

The colon : tells the computer what follows IS the definition, which is ALWAYS indented.

def tells the computer you want to **define** a new function.

This is the **function name**. It shows up **blue** (not **purple** or **black**, like the functions before) because you're defining it.

4. Enter these instructions to create a v-shape. (See what's happening in diagram A on the right.)

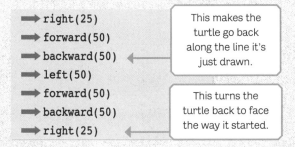

```
right(25)
forward(50)
backward(50)
left(50)
forward(50)
backward(50)
right(25)
```

This makes the turtle go back along the line it's just drawn.

This turns the turtle back to face the way it started.

5. Now start a new function, to turn your v-shape (diagram B) into one 'arm' of the snowflake.

```
def snowflakeArm():
```

6. Enter these intructions. (Diagrams C and D show what's happening now.)

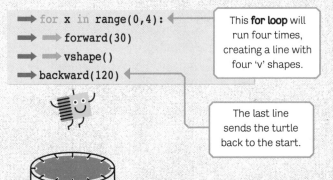

```
for x in range(0,4):
    forward(30)
    vshape()
backward(120)
```

This **for loop** will run four times, creating a line with four 'v' shapes.

The last line sends the turtle back to the start.

CREATING FUNCTIONS

Python has many ready-made functions, such as **print()** and **input()** – but you can also create your own using the keyword **def** (short for define).

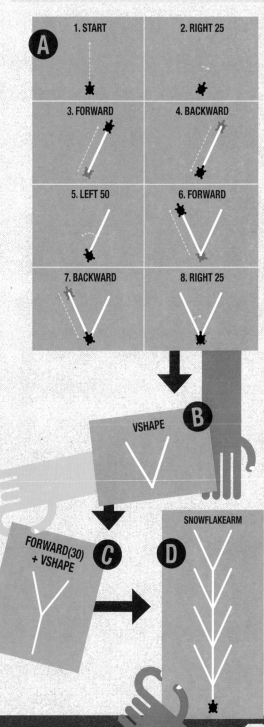

A
1. START	2. RIGHT 25
3. FORWARD	4. BACKWARD
5. LEFT 50	6. FORWARD
7. BACKWARD	8. RIGHT 25

VSHAPE B

FORWARD(30) + VSHAPE C   D SNOWFLAKEARM

49

7. Create another function to draw a whole snowflake, using a **for loop** to repeat the snowflake arm you just made.

```
def snowflake():
    for x in range(0,6):
        snowflakeArm()
        right(60)
```

The **for loop** will run 6 times, creating 6 arms.

This makes the turtle turn 60 degrees before starting the next arm.

8. Finally, call the **snowflake()** function.

```
snowflake()
```

Save and run your program. You should see the **turtle** graphics window pop up and the turtle draw a snowflake, like this:

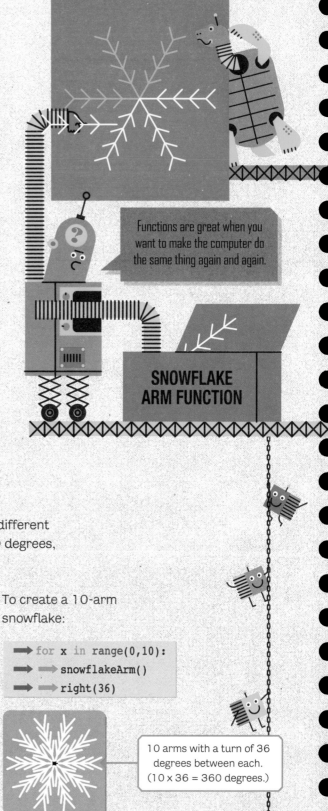

Functions are great when you want to make the computer do the same thing again and again.

SNOWFLAKE ARM FUNCTION

CUSTOMIZE YOUR SNOWFLAKE

You could create different snowflakes by putting in different values in step 7. Make sure the turns add up to 360 degrees, so the snowflake goes all the way around.

To create an 18-arm snowflake:

```
for x in range(0,18):
    snowflakeArm()
    right(20)
```

18 arms with a turn of 20 degrees in between each. (20 x 18 = 360 degrees.)

To create a 10-arm snowflake:

```
for x in range(0,10):
    snowflakeArm()
    right(36)
```

10 arms with a turn of 36 degrees between each. (10 x 36 = 360 degrees.)

FANTASTIC FUNCTIONS

Functions are used a lot in Python. Here are some handy reminders.

- Function names are generally followed by a pair of brackets. You use or **call** a function by typing in its name, followed by the brackets. This is known as a **function call**.

- Python comes with lots of ready-made, built-in functions, such as **print()** and **range()**. These show up **purple**.

- You can access even more functions by importing **modules** – libraries of ready-made functions, such as the **random** and **turtle** modules. These show up **black**.

- You can also create your own functions using **def** (see page 49). One example is **snowflakeArm()**. These show up **blue** when you define them, but **black** when you call them. Home-made functions really come into their own in long programs, helping to break up your code and organise it clearly.

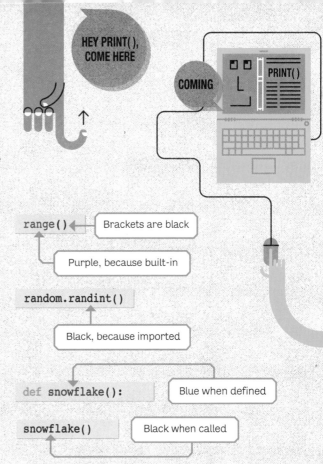

range() ← Brackets are black

Purple, because built-in

random.randint()

Black, because imported

def snowflake(): Blue when defined

snowflake() Black when called

An argument doesn't mean people shouting. It's just a technical word for a type of information.

ARGUMENTS AREN'T ANGRY.

- The brackets after the function name are for **parameters** – variables that you want the function to use. When you call a function, you can set the parameters by putting values inside the brackets. These values are known as **arguments**. For example, **range(0,6)** has the arguments 0 and 6.

- Sometimes, the brackets are left empty. A function with empty brackets should do the same thing every time, like **snowflakeArm()** on the previous page.

- Some functions need to **return a value** – meaning they find or work out a bit of information, then pass it back so your program can use it. For example, **range(0,6)** returns a list: [0,1,2,3,4,5]. The **function call** both runs the function AND represents the information it returns. So you don't need to type anything else.

COLOURED SNOWFLAKES

You can use the **random module** to make a multicoloured snowflake.

1. Open your snowflake program and save it with a new name, then add this at the top:

```
import random
```

2. Delete the line that set the pen colour (so you can use different colours):

```
pencolor("white")
```
← **DELETE** this line.

3. Now you need to set up a list of colours, and insert it after the line where you set the background.

You could include more colours for more variety. (See the list on page 46.)

```
colours = ["blue", "purple", "cyan", "white", "yellow", "green", "orange"]
```

4. Then, pick a colour from the list for each snowflake arm. This means adding an extra line in the **for loop** at the end of your program:

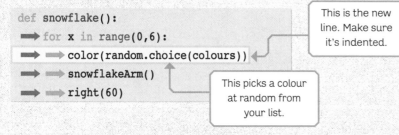
```
def snowflake():
    for x in range(0,6):
        color(random.choice(colours))
        snowflakeArm()
        right(60)
```

This is the new line. Make sure it's indented.

This picks a colour at random from your list.

5. Save and run the program. You should get a multicoloured snowflake.

CREATE A SNOWSTORM

You can also use the **random module** to fill the screen with snowflakes of different sizes.

1. Save your colourful snowflake program, above, with a new name.

Turtles can be a bit slow. So when you run this code, it may take a few minutes (depending on how many snowflakes you ask for).

LET IT SNOW
LET IT SNOW
LET IT...WAIT...

2. To vary the size of the snowflakes, you need to add a 'size' variable to your `snowflake()` function, like this:

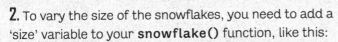

```
def snowflake(size):
    for x in range(0,6):
        color(random.choice(colours))
        snowflakeArm(size)
        right(60)
```

The 'size' variable goes in both sets of brackets.

If you want each snowflake to be a *single* colour, move this above the **for** loop.

3. You also need to add this new 'size' variable to the **vshape()** and **snowflakeArm()** functions, to replace numbers in the **forward** and **backward** commands, like this:

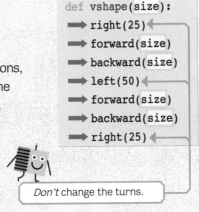

```
def vshape(size):
    right(25)
    forward(size)
    backward(size)
    left(50)
    forward(size)
    backward(size)
    right(25)
```

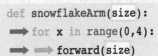

```
def snowflakeArm(size):
    for x in range(0,4):
        forward(size)
        vshape(size)
    backward(size*4)
```

You need to multiply the last one by 4 to send the turtle back to the start.

Don't change the turns.

4. Lastly, replace the final line of your program with a **for loop** to draw several snowflakes, each with its own size and position chosen at random.

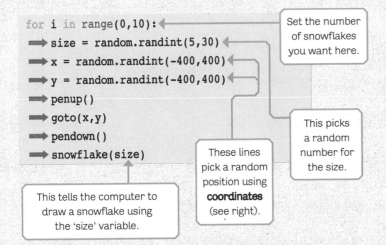

```
for i in range(0,10):
    size = random.randint(5,30)
    x = random.randint(-400,400)
    y = random.randint(-400,400)
    penup()
    goto(x,y)
    pendown()
    snowflake(size)
```

Set the number of snowflakes you want here.

This picks a random number for the size.

These lines pick a random position using **coordinates** (see right).

This tells the computer to draw a snowflake using the 'size' variable.

5. Save and run your code. You should get a small flurry of snowflakes.

USING COORDINATES

You can describe any point on the screen using **coordinates**. The **x-coordinate** tells you how far across it is, and the **y-coordinate** tells you how far up or down.

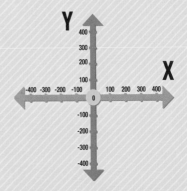

In **turtle**, you can jump straight to certain coordinates using the function **goto(x,y)**. You can do this without leaving a trail if you add **penup()** – just put **pendown()** to start drawing again.

DON'T PRESS THE BUTTON

This program creates a button that will display different messages when someone clicks on it.

TINKERING WITH PICTURES

To make a button that appears on screen, you'll need a Python module called **tkinter** (say 'tee kay inter'). Tkinter is a set of tools that let you create pictures, or **graphics**, on the screen. It was designed for making 'Graphical User Interfaces' (see right).

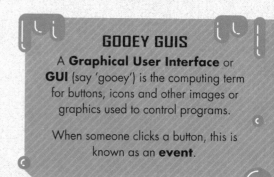

GOOEY GUIS
A **Graphical User Interface** or **GUI** (say 'gooey') is the computing term for buttons, icons and other images or graphics used to control programs.

When someone clicks a button, this is known as an **event**.

1. Open a new file and save it. Then import **tkinter**:

```
import tkinter
```

2. Next, you need to make the computer create a named **tkinter** window.

```
window = tkinter.Tk()
```

We've called it 'window'.

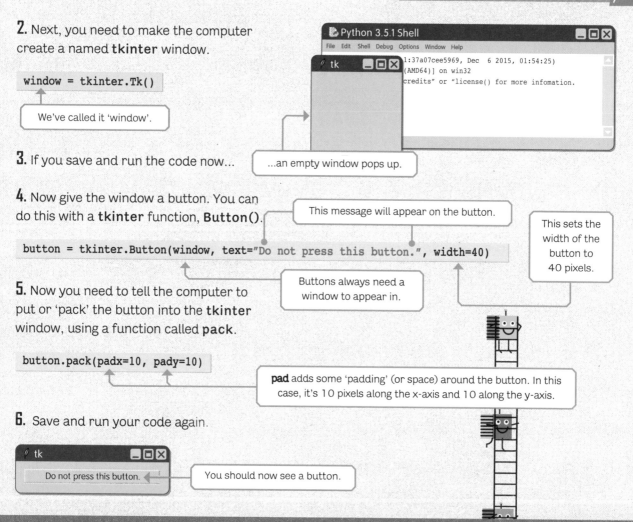

3. If you save and run the code now...

...an empty window pops up.

4. Now give the window a button. You can do this with a **tkinter** function, **Button()**.

This message will appear on the button.

This sets the width of the button to 40 pixels.

```
button = tkinter.Button(window, text="Do not press this button.", width=40)
```

5. Now you need to tell the computer to put or 'pack' the button into the **tkinter** window, using a function called **pack**.

Buttons always need a window to appear in.

```
button.pack(padx=10, pady=10)
```

pad adds some 'padding' (or space) around the button. In this case, it's 10 pixels along the x-axis and 10 along the y-axis.

6. Save and run your code again.

Do not press this button.

You should now see a button.

7. Add a variable, to keep track of how many times the button has been clicked.

```
clickCount = 0
```

The count should start at zero.

GOING GLOBAL

A **global** variable can be used by any part of a program. Variables created outside functions are global. You can access them inside functions using the keyword, **global**. If you create a variable *inside* a function, it can be used ONLY inside that function.

8. Now create a function that tells the computer what to do after each click (the **event**).

```
def onClick(event):
    global clickCount
    clickCount = clickCount + 1
    if clickCount == 1:
        button.configure(text="Seriously? Do. Not. Press. It.")
    elif clickCount == 2:
        button.configure(text="Gah! Next time, no more button.")
    else:
        button.pack_forget()
```

global allows this function to use the variable you just created (see box).

Each time you click, the computer adds one to the counter.

You get different messages appear the first two times you click.

pack_forget() deletes the button.

The **else** statement runs when you click again.

9. To make this work, you need to link or **bind** your function to the act of clicking and releasing the button.

This is the number 1, not the letter 'l'.

```
button.bind("<ButtonRelease-1>", onClick)
```

10. Add a line to make the whole thing run.

```
window.mainloop()
```

This runs the code attached to your window.

Humans! You never obey instructions, do you?

11. Save and run your program. You should get a button with a series of messages, like this:

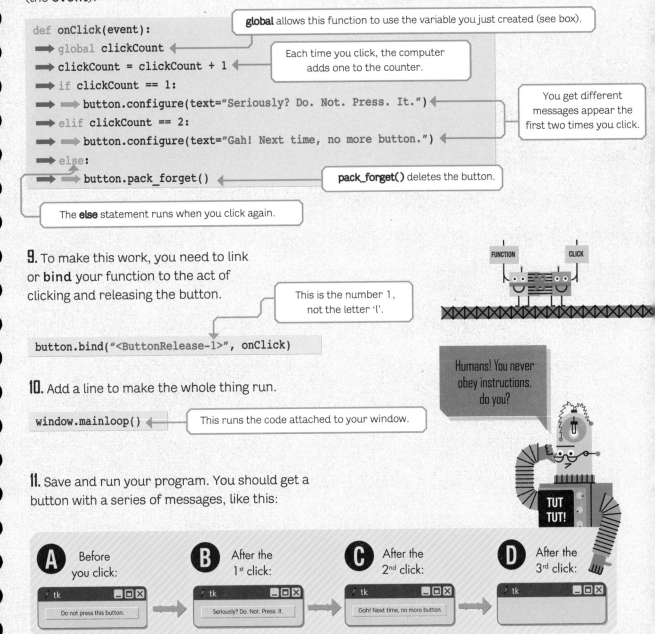

A Before you click:

tk — □ ✕
Do not press this button.

B After the 1st click:

tk — □ ✕
Seriously? Do. Not. Press. It.

C After the 2nd click:

tk — □ ✕
Gah! Next time, no more button.

D After the 3rd click:

tk — □ ✕

TUT TUT!

MAKE A MASTERPIECE

This program allows you to make your own 'paintings' by dragging your **mouse-pointer** around the screen.

PAINTING ON A CANVAS

In **tkinter**, you can create pictures on a **canvas** – a blank backdrop with **x** and **y coordinates** to keep track of where you're drawing.

DRAWING SHAPES

Tkinter has various functions especially for drawing shapes.

create_line() draws a line

create_rectangle() draws a rectangle or a square

create_oval() draws an oval or circle

I. Open and save a new file, then import **tkinter**.

```
import tkinter
```

2. Add a couple of **print()** functions to explain how to use the program.

```
print("To draw, hold down the left mouse button and move your mouse around.")
print("To change your brush colour, click on one of the colours.")
```

> This text will be displayed in the Shell window when the program runs.

3. Now, you need to tell the computer to create a canvas when the program runs.

```
window = tkinter.Tk()
canvas = tkinter.Canvas(window, width=750, height=500, bg="white")
canvas.pack()
```

> This creates a **tkinter** window and gives it a name.

> **pack()** puts the canvas in the **tkinter** window.

> These **arguments** set the size of the canvas in pixels, and its colour.

> This command creates a blank **tkinter canvas**.

> Unlike screen coordinates, *canvas* coordinates start from 0 in the **top left** corner.

4. Create two variables to represent the **x** and **y coordinates** of the mouse pointer. (You can create both at the same time, separated by commas.) To start with, both variables should be 0. Set a starting colour for your paint, too.

```
lastX, lastY = 0,0
colour = "black"
```

This is the top left-hand corner of the canvas.

5. Now create a function to keep track of the mouse-pointer – we called it **store_position()** – so you can draw lines as it moves.

```
def store_position(event):
    global lastX, lastY
    lastX = event.x
    lastY = event.y
```

This allows the function to access the 'lastX' and 'lastY' variables created in step 4.

This keeps track of the **x** and **y** coordinates of the mouse-pointer as it moves.

6. Next, create a function to tell the computer what to do when you click on the canvas. Store the position of the click by calling the **store_position()** function.

The parameter for this function is the **event** of clicking the mouse.

```
def on_click(event):
    store_position(event)
```

This is the function you created in the previous step.

7. Add another function to draw a line when the mouse-pointer is dragged aross the canvas.

This calls the **create_line()** function and runs it on the canvas.

fill allows you to set the colour of the line.

width sets the thickness of the line in pixels (3 is similar to a felt-tip pen).

```
def on_drag(event):
    canvas.create_line(lastX, lastY, event.x, event.y, fill = colour, width = 3)
    store_position(event)
```

This records the position of the mouse-pointer when you *finish* dragging.

These variables contain the coordinates of the pointer when last clicked or dragged (the *start* position).

event.x and **event.y** contain the *current* **x** and **y** coordinates — that is, where the pointer has been dragged to.

PLEASE TURN OVER TO CONTINUE

8. Connect your **on_click()** and **on_drag()** functions to clicks and drags on the canvas using **bind()** (see box).

```
canvas.bind("<Button-1>", on_click)
canvas.bind("<B1-Motion>", on_drag)
```

This binds a left mouse-click to the **on_click()** function. Note the button name is '1' (one), not 'l' for left.

<B1-Motion> means any mouse movement while the left mouse button is pressed. This line binds that action to the **on_drag()** function.

9. Add a line to run your program. Then save and run everything so far, to test it. You should be able to paint, but only in black.

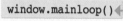
```
window.mainloop()
```

This line needs to stay at the end of the program, so type everything that follows ABOVE it.

BINDING

Tkinter has several functions that allow you to link or **bind** your code to items on the canvas.

canvas.bind() links a function to an **event** (such as a mouse click) on the canvas.

canvas.tag_bind() links an event to an **object** (such as a shape) on the canvas.

10. To paint in colours, you can add a palette of clickable squares. To create and position these on the canvas, you need to use coordinates...

You've already used **screen coordinates** in your **turtle** programs (see page 53). **Canvas coordinates** work in much the same way, but zero comes in a different place.

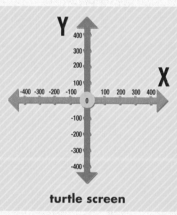

turtle screen **tkinter canvas**

Canvas coordinates get bigger in value as you move right and down.

Add the squares and set their coordinates, like this.

Each square gets its own **id**, which can then be used to identify it (see box).

Each square is outlined using **x** and **y** coordinates.

Left Top Right Bottom
(x) (y) (x)   (y)

fill tells the computer to fill each square with the named colour.

ID

When you create an object (such as a shape) on a canvas, the computer gives it an **id** in order to keep track of it.

For example, **red_id** is the id for your red square.

```
red_id = canvas.create_rectangle(10, 10, 30, 30, fill="red")
blue_id = canvas.create_rectangle(10, 35, 30, 55, fill="blue")
black_id = canvas.create_rectangle(10, 60, 30, 80, fill="black")
white_id = canvas.create_rectangle(10, 85, 30, 105, fill="white")
```

11. To change the paint colour, you will need a separate function for each colour on your palette, like this.

```
def set_colour_red(event):
    global colour
    colour="red"

def set_colour_blue(event):
    global colour
    colour="blue"

def set_colour_black(event):
    global colour
    colour="black"

def set_colour_white(event):
    global colour
    colour="white"
```

The parameter for this function will be the **event** of clicking on the red square.

global allows you to change the global 'colour' variable defined earlier.

White is useful for erasing things.

12. You can use a **tkinter** function called **tag_bind()** to link the act of clicking each square in the palette to your **set_colour** functions.

This means a left mouse-click.

```
canvas.tag_bind(red_id, "<Button-1>", set_colour_red)
canvas.tag_bind(blue_id, "<Button-1>", set_colour_blue)
canvas.tag_bind(black_id, "<Button-1>", set_colour_black)
canvas.tag_bind(white_id, "<Button-1>", set_colour_white)
```

These call the **set_colour** functions you created in the last step.

tag_bind() is used to link an **event** on an **object** (that is, a click on one of your squares) to a particular function.

13. Save and run the program to test it. If you find any bugs, check your spelling, punctuation and spacing. (For more debugging tips, see pages 88-89). Then, try making your own masterpiece.

PRINT SCREEN

If you want to save your painting, press the **PrtScr** button (short for 'print screen'). This copies everything on your screen. Then open an image editing program and press **Control + v** to paste the copied image into it. (On a Mac®, press **Command, Shift + 3** and paste the image into **Preview** with **Control + v**). You can now save it as an image file.

DODGE THE BOMBS

Watch out! Hidden bombs lurk beneath a green field in this puzzle game. Can you find all the safe squares without setting off an explosion?

THE GAME

Here's how the game works and looks when it's finished. The field is divided into squares.

1. When you run the game, a new window pops up in front of the Shell window.

The 'tk' shows this window was created with **tkinter**.

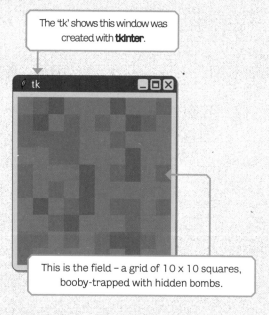

This is the field – a grid of 10 x 10 squares, booby-trapped with hidden bombs.

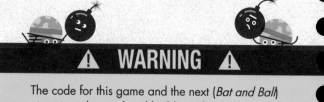

⚠ **WARNING** ⚠

The code for this game and the next (*Bat and Ball*) is quite advanced and builds on the skills you've learned earlier, so make sure you've worked through the rest of the book before you try them.

2. You click on one of the squares to test it. If it is safe, it turns brown and a number appears.

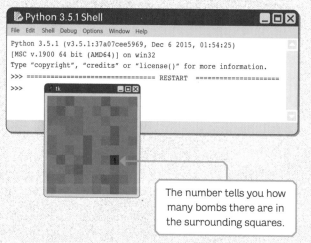

The number tells you how many bombs there are in the surrounding squares.

3. If you hit a bomb, the square turns red and the game ends.

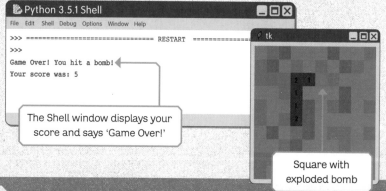

The Shell window displays your score and says 'Game Over!'

Square with exploded bomb

HOW DOES IT WORK?

To make the game work, your program needs to...

- Decide where the bombs go.

- Draw the field full of bombs on the screen.

- React when the player clicks on a square, changing the colour to red for a bomb or, if the square is safe, changing it to brown and revealing the number of bombs around it.

- Keep track of the player's score (how many safe squares they find).

- End the game and show the score if a bomb is hit.

- End the game and congratulate the player if they find all the safe squares.

Here's how that looks as a flow chart.

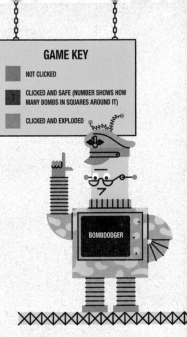

GAME KEY

NOT CLICKED

1 CLICKED AND SAFE (NUMBER SHOWS HOW MANY BOMBS IN SQUARES AROUND IT)

CLICKED AND EXPLODED

PLEASE TURN OVER TO START CODING

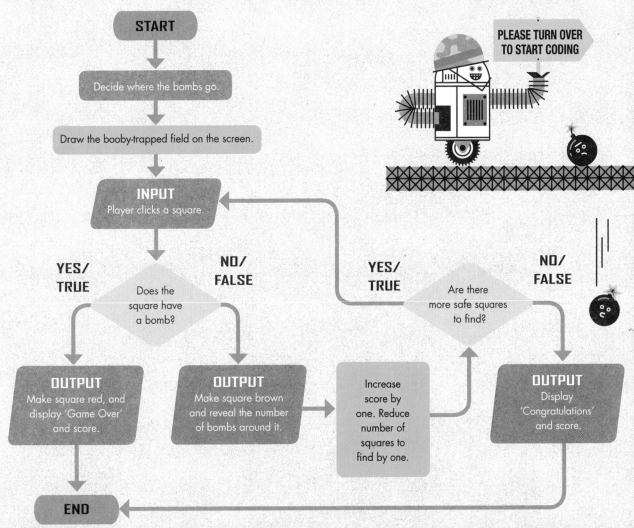

START

Decide where the bombs go.

Draw the booby-trapped field on the screen.

INPUT
Player clicks a square.

Does the square have a bomb?

YES/ TRUE   **NO/ FALSE**

OUTPUT
Make square red, and display 'Game Over' and score.

OUTPUT
Make square brown and reveal the number of bombs around it.

Increase score by one. Reduce number of squares to find by one.

Are there more safe squares to find?

YES/ TRUE   **NO/ FALSE**

OUTPUT
Display 'Congratulations' and score.

END

CREATING YOUR FIELD

To draw the field, you need to use the **tkinter** module. You also need the **random** module, to lay out the bombs at random.

1. Open and save a new Code window file. Then, import the **tkinter** module and the **random** module.

```
import tkinter
import random
```

Hmmm, where shall I put these?

RANDOM

2. Next, you need to create some variables to keep track of whether the game is over, the score (the number of squares clicked), and how many squares are left to clear.

```
gameOver = False
score = 0
squaresToClear = 0
```

'gameOver' will tell the computer when the game ends. It must be set to **False** for the game to begin.

TRUE AND FALSE
In coding, **true** and **false** are used so computers can make decisions. Remember, computers can *only* answer simple true/false questions. This is known as **Boolean Logic** (see page 16).

3. Now you can tell the computer what your program will do. (Doing this first helps with planning, and means you don't have to worry about the order in which you define things.)

```
def play_bombdodger():
    create_bombfield(bombfield)
    window = tkinter.Tk()
    layout_window(window)
    window.mainloop()
```

When you play the game, the computer will...

...create a booby-trapped field...

...bring up a **tkinter** graphics window and draw the field in it...

...run the game.

The functions inside **play_bombdodger()** will be defined later. This function just tells the computer in what order to call them.

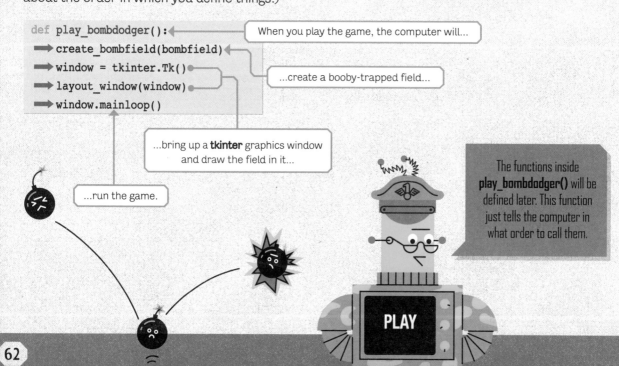

PLAY

PLANTING THE BOMBS

For the computer to remember where the bombs are, you use a grid of numbers: 1 for a bomb, and 0 for a safe square. You can lay out the grid using **lists**.

You've already used simple lists to store information. For more complex information like this, it's faster to use lists *inside* lists. The first list ('bombfield') contains a list of rows. Each row is another list ('rowList') containing the entries for each column in that row.

I'm making a list of lists...

KEY:
BOMB = 1
SAFE = 0

ROW LIST	CONTENTS OF ROW
0	0, 1, 0, 0, 0, 0, 1, 0, 0, 0
1	0, 0, 1, 0, 1, 0, 0, 0, 1, 0
2	0, 0, 1, 0, 0, 0, 1, 0, 0, 0
3	0, 0, 0, 0, 0, 0, 1, 1, 0, 0

4. You need to start with an empty list, then create a **function** to fill it. The same function will also need to update how many squares are left to clear.

You could leave a blank line before the start of a new function if you want to break up your code.

```
bombfield = []
def create_bombfield(bombfield):
    global squaresToClear
```

This creates a list called 'bombfield'.

global tells the computer to use the 'global' variable which you set up at the start.

5. Now, complete the **function**. First use a **for loop** to set up ten empty lists (the rows). Then add another **for loop** to run once for each list, filling it with 0s and 1s. (You can use a random number generator to decide what goes where.)

```
for row in range(0,10):
    rowList = []
    for column in range(0,10):
        if random.randint(1,100) < 20:
            rowList.append(1)
        else:
            rowList.append(0)
            squaresToClear = squaresToClear + 1
    bombfield.append(rowList)
```

This **for loop** runs 10 times...

...creating an empty list (or row) each time.

Inside every row list, another **for loop** adds 10 numbers (or columns).

This generates a random number from 1-100. *If* the number is less than 20, the computer adds a 1 (bomb) to the 'rowList'...

...otherwise, it adds a 0 (safe square) to the 'rowList' AND adds 1 to 'squaresToClear'.

This attaches each finished 'rowList' to the original list.

6. It would be handy to look at your lists, to check your code so far is working. This means adding a **print()** function.

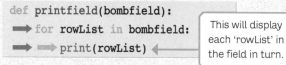

> When this runs, it will display the lists in the Shell window.

(If you leave this line in when you play, you will see a map of the bombs in the Shell window.)

7. Then define the function, so it displays the contents of the lists.

```
def printfield(bombfield):
    for rowList in bombfield:
        print(rowList)
```

> This will display each 'rowList' in the field in turn.

8. Save and run the program so far to test it. Add a line to call your **play_bombdodger** function, then save and run your code. This will become the last line of your program.

```
play_bombdodger()
```

> Type the code for step 9 **ABOVE** this line.

You should see a blank **tkinter** window pop up, and a grid of 0s and 1s will appear in the Shell window. You will also get an error message, which you will fix in the next step.

TESTING

With longer programs, it's a good idea to check it as you go along. Adding a **print()** function is one way to *see* what your code is doing and spot any bugs.

Add **#** to the start of **printfield()** once you finish testing. This stops it running by turning it into a **comment** – a note coders leave in the code for other coders.

> Blank **tkinter** window

> Each 0 represents a safe square, each 1 is a bomb.

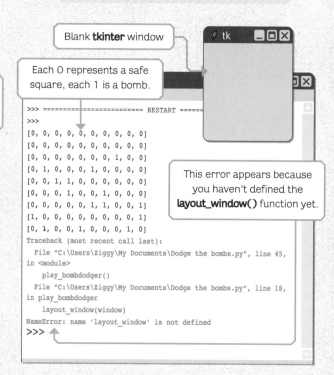

```
>>> ======================= RESTART ======
>>>
[0, 0, 0, 0, 0, 0, 0, 0, 0, 0]
[0, 0, 0, 0, 0, 0, 0, 0, 0, 0]
[0, 0, 0, 0, 0, 0, 0, 1, 0, 0]
[0, 1, 0, 0, 0, 1, 0, 0, 0, 0]
[0, 0, 1, 1, 0, 0, 0, 0, 0, 0]
[0, 0, 0, 1, 0, 0, 1, 0, 0, 0]
[0, 0, 0, 0, 0, 1, 1, 0, 0, 1]
[1, 0, 0, 0, 0, 0, 0, 0, 0, 1]
[0, 1, 0, 0, 1, 0, 0, 0, 1, 0]
Traceback (most recent call last):
  File "C:\Users\Ziggy\My Documents\Dodge the bombs.py", line 45,
in <module>
    play_bombdodger()
  File "C:\Users\Ziggy\My Documents\Dodge the bombs.py", line 18,
in play_bombdodger
    layout_window(window)
NameError: name 'layout_window' is not defined
>>>
```

> This error appears because you haven't defined the **layout_window()** function yet.

9. Next, you need to lay out the squares in the window by defining the **layout_window()** function. Start by telling the computer to look at each entry in your lists, using **for loops** and a function called **enumerate()**. (See below.)

> This is the **tkinter** window that pops up when you run the game.

> The *outer* **for loop** goes down the rows.

> The *inner* **for loop** goes through the columns.

```
def layout_window(window):
    for rowNumber, rowList in enumerate(bombfield):
        for columnNumber, columnEntry in enumerate(rowList):
```

> **enumerate()** finds the index numbers for the items in each 'rowList' and pairs each index number with its item. This makes it easier for the computer to look up parts of the list.

> ENUMERATE()

ENUMERATE()

enumerate() is a function that goes through each item in a list and **returns** both the index and the item.

10. Now, make the function randomly generate colours for each square. You will also add a blank label, to make the squares the right size.

The mix of greens helps you to see where the different squares are.

if statement
IF the random number is below 25, the square will be dark green.

elif statement
Or ELSE IF the random number is over 75, the square will be sea green.

else statement
Or ELSE for any other number, the square will be just green.

```
if random.randint(1,100) < 25:
        square = tkinter.Label(window, text = "    ", bg = "darkgreen")
    elif random.randint(1,100) > 75:
        square = tkinter.Label(window, text = "    ", bg = "seagreen")
    else:
        square = tkinter.Label(window, text = "    ", bg = "green")
```

bg stands for background.

Use commas to separate **parameters**.

tkinter.Label() creates a label box (which forms the square).

This links the square to the **tk window** you made earlier.

Type four spaces between the quotation marks. This will be the width of the square.

GREAT GRIDS

grid() divides the **tkinter** window into a grid of rows and columns. Once you've got a grid, you can also use other grid functions, such as…

grid_info() pulls information out of the grid and turns it into a **dictionary**, so you can look up things like rows and columns quickly.

11. Now you need to tell the computer to lay out each square in turn, in a grid inside the **tkinter** window. For this, you will need a new function, **grid()**.

```
square.grid(row = rowNumber, column = columnNumber)
```

The . means the **grid()** function which follows belongs to the square.

The **grid()** function has lots of built-in parameters. For the position of the square, you just need **row** and **column**.

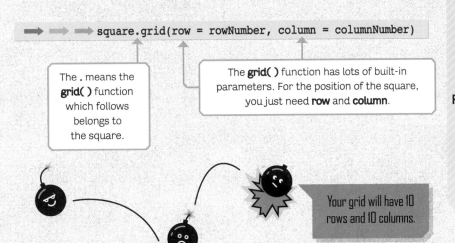

ROWS

COLUMNS

Your grid will have 10 rows and 10 columns.

12. Test everything is working by saving and running the program. Make sure this line is at the bottom of your code:

```
play_bombdodger()
```

This line must stay at the end of your program, because computers read from top to bottom – and you need to define everything *before* you play.

PLAY

You should see a window pop up, like this:

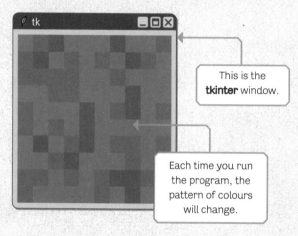

tk

This is the **tkinter** window.

Each time you run the program, the pattern of colours will change.

Don't worry if you get some errors. People often do, in a long program like this.

Going back and fixing errors is a good way of learning more about how Python works!

You should also see a map of the bombs in the Shell window:

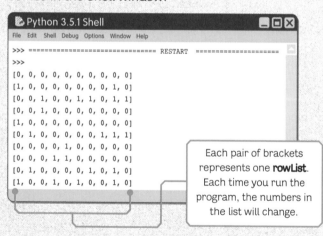

```
Python 3.5.1 Shell
File  Edit  Shell  Debug  Options  Window  Help
>>> ========================= RESTART =========================
>>>
[0, 0, 0, 0, 0, 0, 0, 0, 0, 0]
[1, 0, 0, 0, 0, 0, 0, 0, 1, 0]
[0, 0, 1, 0, 0, 1, 1, 0, 1, 1]
[0, 0, 1, 0, 0, 0, 0, 0, 0, 0]
[1, 0, 0, 0, 0, 0, 0, 0, 0, 0]
[0, 1, 0, 0, 0, 0, 0, 1, 1, 1]
[0, 0, 0, 0, 1, 0, 0, 0, 0, 0]
[0, 0, 0, 1, 1, 0, 0, 0, 0, 0]
[0, 1, 0, 0, 0, 0, 1, 0, 1, 0]
[1, 0, 0, 1, 0, 1, 0, 0, 1, 0]
```

Each pair of brackets represents one **rowList**. Each time you run the program, the numbers in the list will change.

DEBUGGING

If you get an error message, it will say which line (or lines) of code to check. If you can't spot an error, check the line *above* too.

• Have you closed all the brackets? If you miss a bracket, Python will report an error in the following line, because of how it reads code.

• Have you spelled all the words correctly?

• Are your indents correct?

See page 71 and pages 88-89 for more debugging tips.

13. If everything is working, you can turn off the **print()** function you added in step 6... unless you want to cheat.

```
#printfield(bombfield)
```

Adding **#** turns the line into a **comment**, so it won't run.

It's easy to win if you have a map!

MAP

REACTING TO A MOUSE CLICK

Now you have a minefield, the next step is to make it react when the player clicks on a square, creating an **event**. **Tkinter** has specific commands to make the computer recognize different events.

EVENT

In computing, an **event** is something that happens, that a program will recognize. That usually means a signal from a user, such as a mouse-click or key-press.

14. You can make the computer recognize a left mouse-button click with **<Button-1>**. You also need to tell the computer *what* to do when this happens AND link all of this to the square. This means adding another line below the line from step 11 (which laid out the squares).

> This is the line you already wrote in step 10.

```
square.grid(row = rowNumber, column = columnNumber)
square.bind("<Button-1>", on_click)
```

bind() links the **event** (the mouse-click) and the computer's **response** (a new function called **on_click()**) to the square.

This is '1' (one) not 'l' (as in left).

Each time you click, a function named **on_click()** will run. (You'll create this function next.)

15. Your last function needs to tell the computer what to do when a square is clicked – which involves using the variables you made earlier.

```
def on_click(event):
    global score
    global gameOver
    global squaresToClear
```

event refers to the click on the square.

The **global** command allows this function to change these variables – even though the variables were created *outside* this function.

16. First, you need to make sure the computer knows *which* square it's looking at. For this, you need a new word: **widget**, meaning 'thingy', to stand for the thing that's been clicked. Then, you need to look up the square's grid position.

This creates a variable called 'square', to represent the thing that has had an event (that is, the square you clicked).

```
square = event.widget
row = int(square.grid_info()["row"])
column = int(square.grid_info()["column"])
```

square.grid_info() pulls out information about the square from the grid (here, the row and column). **int()** makes sure the computer treats that information as a number.

17. Then, you want the computer to check the label text in the square (even if it's just spaces). For this, you need a new function, **cget()**.

```
currentText = square.cget("text")
```

This is a new variable to represent the square's text.

cget("text") looks up the existing text.

SEEING WITH A 'C'

In **tkinter**, **cget()** stands for 'configuration-get' – which is computer-speak for looking up something's settings. You can think of the 'C' as a way of 'see'-ing.

18. Now, check the game is still going. If it is, check for a bomb – and tell the computer what to do if it finds one.

```
if gameOver == False:
    if bombfield[row][column] == 1:
        gameOver = True
        square.config(bg = "red")
        print("Game Over! You hit a bomb!")
        print("Your score was:", score)
```

This checks for a bomb (1 = mine, 0 = safe).

This ends the game.

This turns the square red.

These lines display messages in the Shell window. 'score' is the number of squares clicked beore you died.

19. Then, tell the computer what to do if the square is safe. First, you need to check it hasn't been clicked already. If it hasn't, you want to make it brown and display the number of bombs in the surrounding squares.

```
    elif currentText == "    ":
        square.config(bg = "brown")
        totalBombs = 0
```

If this still contains four spaces, the square has not yet been clicked.

To count the bombs around this square, you need to create a new variable and set it to zero. (You'll do the counting in the next step.)

Phew, you're safe... for now.

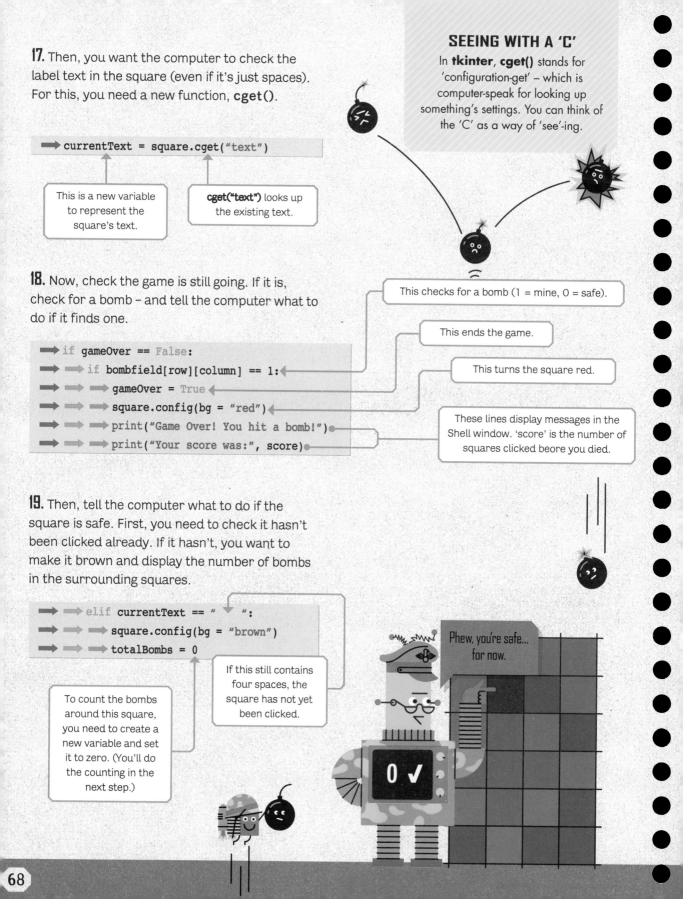

20. To find the number of bombs, you need to check the eight surrounding squares in turn...

Start by checking the square below.

> If you're on the bottom row (row 9) you don't need to check below.

> Look back at the grid on page 65 if you need a reminder of the row and column numbers.

Look back at the grid on page 65 if you need a reminder of the row and column numbers.

BOMB BUGS
Take care with your **operators** – if they're wrong, the game will still run but you'll get the wrong numbers in the brown squares.

```
if row < 9:
    if bombfield[row+1][column] == 1:
        totalBombs = totalBombs + 1
```

> If there *is* a bomb below, the computer adds 1 to the total number of bombs.

Then check the square above.

```
if row > 0:
    if bombfield[row-1][column] == 1:
        totalBombs = totalBombs + 1
```

> If you're on the top row (row 0) you can skip this.

Next, check the square on the left.

```
if column > 0:
    if bombfield[row][column-1] == 1:
        totalBombs = totalBombs + 1
```

> If you're on the left edge (column 0) you can skip this.

Then, check the square on the right.

```
if column < 9:
    if bombfield[row][column+1] == 1:
        totalBombs = totalBombs + 1
```

> If you're on the right edge (column 9) you can skip this.

After that, check the square in the top left corner.

```
if row > 0 and column > 0:
    if bombfield[row-1][column-1] == 1:
        totalBombs = totalBombs + 1
```

> If you're on the top row (row 0) OR left edge (column 0) you can skip this.

Then, check the bottom left corner.

```
if row < 9 and column > 0:
    if bombfield[row+1][column-1] == 1:
        totalBombs = totalBombs + 1
```

> If you're on the bottom row (row 9) OR left edge (column 0) you can skip this.

PLEASE TURN OVER TO CONTINUE

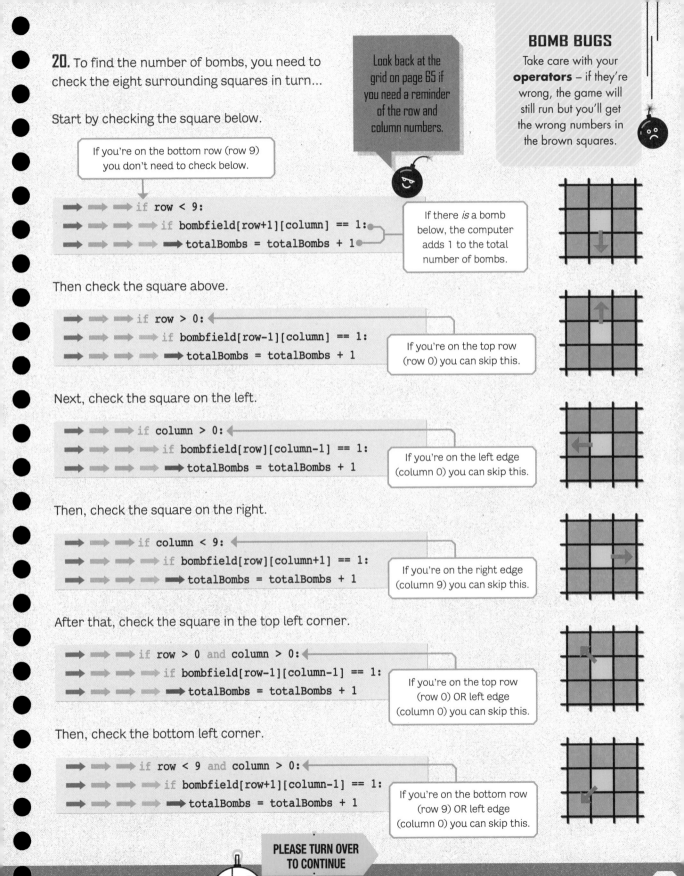

Now, check the square in the top right corner.

```
➡ ➡ ➡ if row > 0 and column < 9:
➡ ➡ ➡ ➡ if bombfield[row-1][column+1] == 1:
➡ ➡ ➡ ➡ totalBombs = totalBombs + 1
```

If you're on the top row (row 0) OR right edge (column 9) you can skip this.

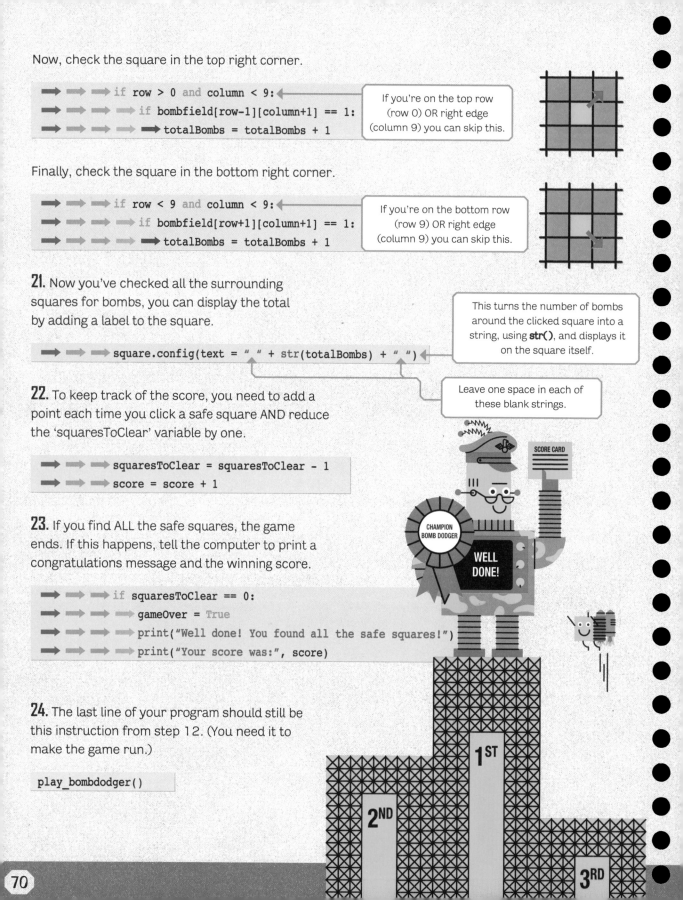

Finally, check the square in the bottom right corner.

```
➡ ➡ ➡ if row < 9 and column < 9:
➡ ➡ ➡ ➡ if bombfield[row+1][column+1] == 1:
➡ ➡ ➡ ➡ totalBombs = totalBombs + 1
```

If you're on the bottom row (row 9) OR right edge (column 9) you can skip this.

21. Now you've checked all the surrounding squares for bombs, you can display the total by adding a label to the square.

This turns the number of bombs around the clicked square into a string, using **str()**, and displays it on the square itself.

```
➡ ➡ ➡ square.config(text = " " + str(totalBombs) + " ")
```

Leave one space in each of these blank strings.

22. To keep track of the score, you need to add a point each time you click a safe square AND reduce the 'squaresToClear' variable by one.

```
➡ ➡ ➡ squaresToClear = squaresToClear - 1
➡ ➡ ➡ score = score + 1
```

23. If you find ALL the safe squares, the game ends. If this happens, tell the computer to print a congratulations message and the winning score.

```
➡ ➡ ➡ if squaresToClear == 0:
➡ ➡ ➡ ➡ gameOver = True
➡ ➡ ➡ ➡ print("Well done! You found all the safe squares!")
➡ ➡ ➡ ➡ print("Your score was:", score)
```

24. The last line of your program should still be this instruction from step 12. (You need it to make the game run.)

```
play_bombdodger()
```

25. You're finished! The full code is shown below. Save and run your program to test it. (If you get any error messages, use the debugging checklist next to step 12.)

```
import tkinter
import random
gameOver = False
score = 0
squaresToClear = 0
def play_bombdodger():
    create_bombfield(bombfield)
    window = tkinter.Tk()
    layout_window(window)
    window.mainloop()
bombfield = []
def create_bombfield(bombfield):
    global squaresToClear
    for row in range(0,10):
        rowList = []
        for column in range(0,10):
            if random.randint(1,100) <20:
                rowList.append(1)
            else:
                rowList.append(0)
                squaresToClear = squaresToClear + 1
        bombfield.append(rowList)
    #printfield(bombfield)
def printfield(bombfield):
    for rowList in bombfield:
        print(rowList)
play_bombdodger()
def layout_window(window):
    for rowNumber, rowList in enumerate(bombfield):
        for columnNumber, columnEntry in enumerate(rowList):
            if random.randint(1,100) < 25:
                square = tkinter.Label(window, text = "      ", bg = "darkgreen")
            elif random.randint(1,100) > 75:
                square = tkinter.Label(window, text = "      ", bg = "seagreen")
            else:
                square = tkinter.Label(window, text = "      ", bg = "green")
            square.grid(row = rowNumber, column = columnNumber)
            square.bind("<Button-1>", on_click)
play_bombdodger()
def on_click(event):
    global score
    global gameOver
    global squaresToClear
    square = event.widget
    row = int(square.grid_info()["row"])
```

When *not* a comment, this prints a map of the bombs in the Shell window.

The greyed-out line shows where this goes in step 8.

The greyed-out line shows where this goes in step 11.

It's safe to click on ALL the squares surrounding a 0 square.

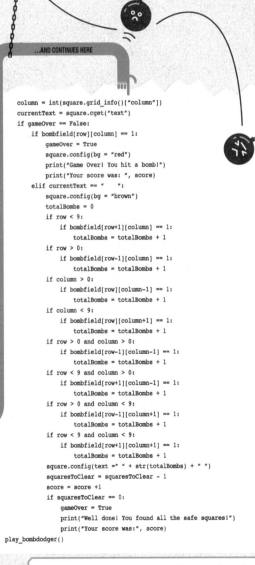

THE CODE FOLLOWS ON FROM HERE...

...AND CONTINUES HERE

```
    column = int(square.grid_info()["column"])
    currentText = square.cget("text")
    if gameOver == False:
        if bombfield[row][column] == 1:
            gameOver = True
            square.config(bg = "red")
            print("Game Over! You hit a bomb!")
            print("Your score was: ", score)
        elif currentText == "      ":
            square.config(bg = "brown")
            totalBombs = 0
            if row < 9:
                if bombfield[row+1][column] == 1:
                    totalBombs = totalBombs + 1
            if row > 0:
                if bombfield[row-1][column] == 1:
                    totalBombs = totalBombs + 1
            if column > 0:
                if bombfield[row][column-1] == 1:
                    totalBombs = totalBombs + 1
            if column < 9:
                if bombfield[row][column+1] == 1:
                    totalBombs = totalBombs + 1
            if row > 0 and column > 0:
                if bombfield[row-1][column-1] == 1:
                    totalBombs = totalBombs + 1
            if row < 9 and column > 0:
                if bombfield[row+1][column-1] == 1:
                    totalBombs = totalBombs + 1
            if row > 0 and column < 9:
                if bombfield[row-1][column+1] == 1:
                    totalBombs = totalBombs + 1
            if row < 9 and column < 9:
                if bombfield[row+1][column+1] == 1:
                    totalBombs = totalBombs + 1
            square.config(text =" " + str(totalBombs) + " ")
            squaresToClear = squaresToClear - 1
            score = score +1
            if squaresToClear == 0:
                gameOver = True
                print("Well done! You found all the safe squares!")
                print("Your score was:", score)
play_bombdodger()
```

You can see a complete, working version of this program online. Just go to **www.usborne.com/quicklinks** and type in the name of this book, plus the page number.

USING PRINTFIELD

You can double-check the maths in your program using the **printfield()** function from step 6. Use this to create a bomb map in the Shell window, then click on all the safe squares, checking if the numbers that appear match the number of bombs. If they *don't* match, check your operators, especially in the code for step 20.

BAT AND BALL

You can use **tkinter** to create a simple bat and ball game –
then see how long you can keep the ball up in the air.

THE GAME

Here's how the game will look when it's finished.

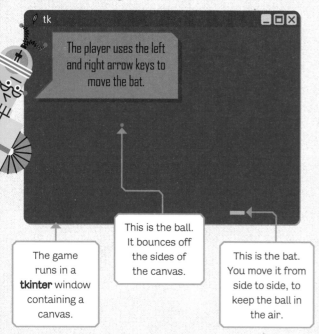

The player uses the left and right arrow keys to move the bat.

The game runs in a **tkinter** window containing a canvas.

This is the ball. It bounces off the sides of the canvas.

This is the bat. You move it from side to side, to keep the ball in the air.

HOW IT WORKS

To make the game work, your program needs to...

- Create shapes for the bat and ball.
- Keep the bat and ball moving.
- Decide when the ball should bounce.
- Stop the game if the ball hits the bottom, and offer the player another go.

To stop the game running too fast, you can add pauses using a module called **time**.

TIME MODULE

The **time** module is often used for information about times and dates. It also allows you to add pauses.

CREATING THE CANVAS, BAT AND BALL

1. Open and save a new file. Import the **tkinter** and **time** modules.

```
import tkinter
import time
```

2. Next, create your canvas.

```
canvasWidth = 750
canvasHeight = 500
window = tkinter.Tk()
canvas = tkinter.Canvas(window, width=canvasWidth, height=canvasHeight, bg="dodgerblue4")
canvas.pack()
```

You need to specify the exact size of the canvas, in pixels, so you can use the measurements to make the ball bounce.

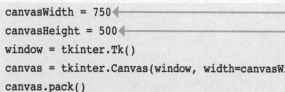

3. You can make a bat using the `create_rectangle()` function. To make a ball, use `create_oval()`. For each shape, you can set the size and colour by filling in the parameters, like this:

create_rectangle() and create_oval() are **tkinter** functions.	Left (X)	Top (Y)	Right (X)	Bottom (Y)

This will make a rectangular turquoise bat, 40 pixels across and 10 pixels high.

```
bat = canvas.create_rectangle(0, 0, 40, 10, fill="dark turquoise")
ball = canvas.create_oval(0, 0, 10, 10, fill="deep pink")
```

These numbers are *temporary* **coordinates**, just to set the size of the shapes. You'll set their starting positions on the canvas later.

This will make a round pink ball, 10 pixels across and 10 pixels high.

COORDINATES AND SHAPES

For a rectangle, the **x** and **y** values give the position of the left, top, right and bottom edges.

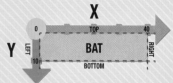

For a round shape, the **x** and **y** values give the position of the left, top, right and bottom points.

4. Set up a variable to keep track of the **tkinter** window.

```
windowOpen = True
```

This will be used to check the **tkinter** window hasn't been closed. It must be set to 'True' for the game to run.

Now you can create the **main loop** – the loop that will handle all the changes while you play. (You will define all of the new functions used here in the next steps.)

Part of the **main_loop()** function's job is to call other functions.

```
def main_loop():
    while windowOpen == True:
        move_bat()
        move_ball()
        window.update()
        time.sleep(0.02)
        if windowOpen == True:
            check_game_over()
```

This will move the bat.

This will move the ball.

You need to check if the window is *still* open after each update.

This updates the **tkinter** window, so you see the objects on the screen move. It also checks for **events** (such as key presses).

This adds a slight pause, to stop the game from running too fast to play.

UPDATE()

Even if the computer is constantly changing something's position, you only SEE it move when the picture on screen is updated – which is why you need **update()**. If the updates happen quickly, it will look as if it's moving smoothly – although it's really a series of static pictures.

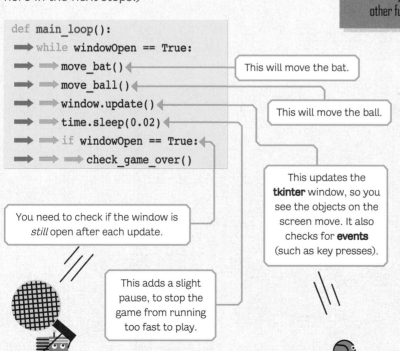

USING ARROW KEYS

5. Type this, to set up a couple of variables. The variables will store information about which arrow key has been pressed.

```
leftPressed = 0
rightPressed = 0
```

0 means *not* pressed; **1** will mean pressed.

These variables will be **global** because they aren't inside a function.

Then create a function to *change* the variables if an arrow key is pressed.

```
def on_key_press(event):
    global leftPressed, rightPressed
    if event.keysym == "Left":
        leftPressed = 1
    elif event.keysym == "Right":
        rightPressed = 1
```

event.keysym links a particular key to an event. **keysym** is short for 'key symbol' – the official names for various keys. These are written as strings: **"Left"** is the left arrow key and **"Right"** is the right arrow key.

If a key is pressed, its variable changes to 1 – which you can use to make the bat move in step 8.

6. The computer also needs to know what to do when a key is released.

```
def on_key_release(event):
    global leftPressed, rightPressed
    if event.keysym == "Left":
        leftPressed = 0
    elif event.keysym == "Right":
        rightPressed = 0
```

When a key is released, its variable goes back to zero.

MOVING THE BAT

7. The bat can only move left or right, so only its **x-coordinate** will change. You can use a variable, 'batMove', to represent this movement. Then you need a formula to change the variable, depending on which arrow key has been pressed.

MOVING SIDEWAYS ON A CANVAS

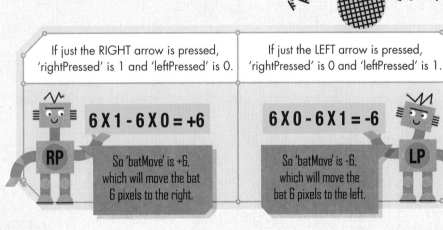

X

0   1   2   3   4

-
If the movement is negative, you are moving LEFT.

+
If the movement is positive, you are moving RIGHT.

'batSpeed' is the number of pixels the bat moves each time the screen updates.

If the RIGHT arrow key is pressed, the movement will be POSITIVE. (If it's not pressed you get zero.)

If the LEFT arrow is pressed, the movement will be NEGATIVE. (If it's not pressed, you get zero.)

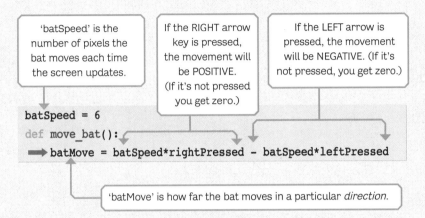

```
batSpeed = 6
def move_bat():
    batMove = batSpeed*rightPressed - batSpeed*leftPressed
```

'batMove' is how far the bat moves in a particular *direction*.

'batSpeed' is always 6, but the value of 'batMove' changes, depending on which direction the bat is moving. The computer works it out like this:

If just the RIGHT arrow is pressed, 'rightPressed' is 1 and 'leftPressed' is 0.

If just the LEFT arrow is pressed, 'rightPressed' is 0 and 'leftPressed' is 1.

RP

$6 \times 1 - 6 \times 0 = +6$

So 'batMove' is +6, which will move the bat 6 pixels to the right.

$6 \times 0 - 6 \times 1 = -6$

So 'batMove' is -6, which will move the bat 6 pixels to the left.

LP

8. Create some variables for the edges of the bat, and use a function called **coords()** (see right) so the computer can tell where the bat is.

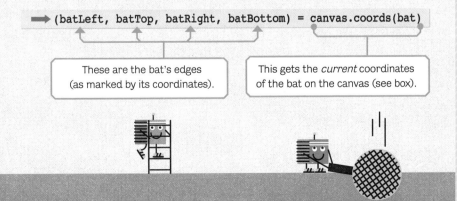

```
(batLeft, batTop, batRight, batBottom) = canvas.coords(bat)
```

These are the bat's edges (as marked by its coordinates).

This gets the *current* coordinates of the bat on the canvas (see box).

COORDS()

You can use the function **coords()** to find out where an object is on a canvas, like this:

canvas.coords()

The object you want to locate goes inside the brackets. The function sends back or **returns** the coordinates, so they can be used by the rest of your program.

9. The bat can only move as long as it stays on the canvas. If it hits the side, it can only go back the other way. You can use an **if/and statement** to stop the bat at the left or right edges.

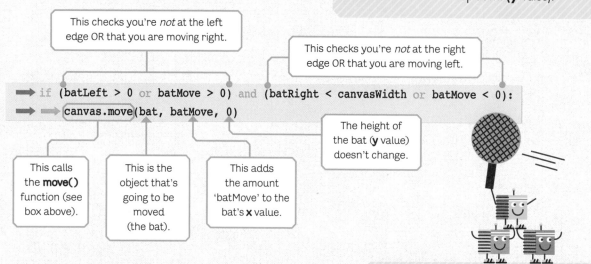

MOVE()

A **tkinter** function called **move()** allows you to move objects on a canvas. It has three **parameters**: the thing you're moving, how much to move it left-right (**x** value), and how much up-down (**y** value).

This checks you're *not* at the left edge OR that you are moving right.

This checks you're *not* at the right edge OR that you are moving left.

```
if (batLeft > 0 or batMove > 0) and (batRight < canvasWidth or batMove < 0):
    canvas.move(bat, batMove, 0)
```

This calls the **move()** function (see box above).

This is the object that's going to be moved (the bat).

This adds the amount 'batMove' to the bat's **x** value.

The height of the bat (**y** value) doesn't change.

A BOUNCING BALL

The ball's movements are more varied. It can move around the whole canvas, bouncing off the top and sides. So *both* its **x** and **y** coordinates will change – represented by two variables: 'ballMoveX' (the ball's left/right movements) and 'ballMoveY' (the ball's up/down movements).

For example, at the start of the game, the ball bounces diagonally up and right like this, meaning…

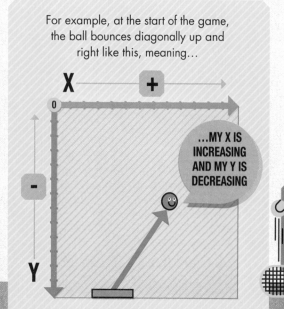

…MY X IS INCREASING AND MY Y IS DECREASING

MOVING ALL OVER A CANVAS

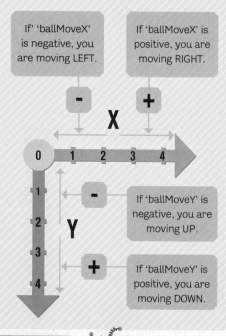

If 'ballMoveX' is negative, you are moving LEFT.

If 'ballMoveX' is positive, you are moving RIGHT.

− X +

0 1 2 3 4

−

Y

+

If 'ballMoveY' is negative, you are moving UP.

If 'ballMoveY' is positive, you are moving DOWN.

The ball will keep moving in the same direction until it hits either the edge of the canvas or the bat.

10. Set up global variables to represent the ball's speed.
You'll also need global variables for the height of the bat.

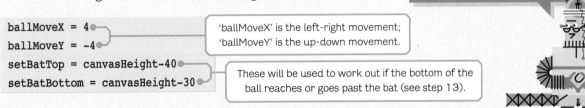

The ball needs TWO variables, because you need to keep track of its movements both left-right (**x** axis) and up-down (**y** axis).

```
ballMoveX = 4
ballMoveY = -4
setBatTop = canvasHeight-40
setBatBottom = canvasHeight-30
```

'ballMoveX' is the left-right movement; 'ballMoveY' is the up-down movement.

These will be used to work out if the bottom of the ball reaches or goes past the bat (see step 13).

11. Now create a function to move the ball.
The function should change the 'ballMove' variables when the ball bounces.
To work out when the ball will bounce, use **coords()** to find the ball's edges.

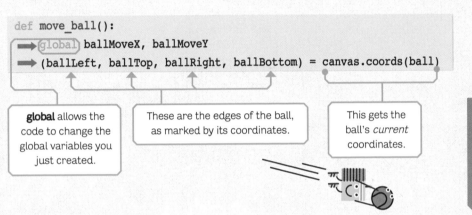

```
def move_ball():
    global ballMoveX, ballMoveY
    (ballLeft, ballTop, ballRight, ballBottom) = canvas.coords(ball)
```

global allows the code to change the global variables you just created.

These are the edges of the ball, as marked by its coordinates.

This gets the ball's *current* coordinates.

Remember 'ballMoveX' doesn't just store how fast the ball is moving (4), but in what *direction* (+4 or -4).

12. When the ball hits the *right* edge of the canvas, it should bounce left (making 'ballMoveX' negative).

If 'ballMoveX' is greater than 0, the ball is moving RIGHT.

This checks if the ball has reached the right edge.

```
if ballMoveX > 0 and ballRight > canvasWidth:
    ballMoveX = -ballMoveX
```

Making 'ballMoveX' negative sends the ball back to the left. The value of 'ballSpeedY' stays the same.

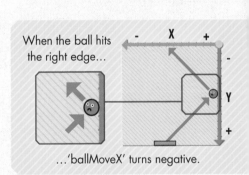

When the ball hits the right edge…

…'ballMoveX' turns negative.

When the ball hits the *left* edge, it should bounce right (making 'ballMoveX' positive).

If 'ballMoveX' is less than 0, the ball is moving LEFT.

This checks if the ball has reached the left edge.

```
if ballMoveX < 0 and ballLeft < 0:
    ballMoveX = -ballMoveX
```

This turns a negative 'ballMoveX' positive again.

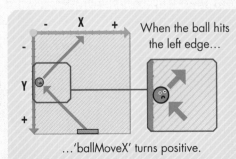

When the ball hits the left edge…

…'ballMoveX' turns positive.

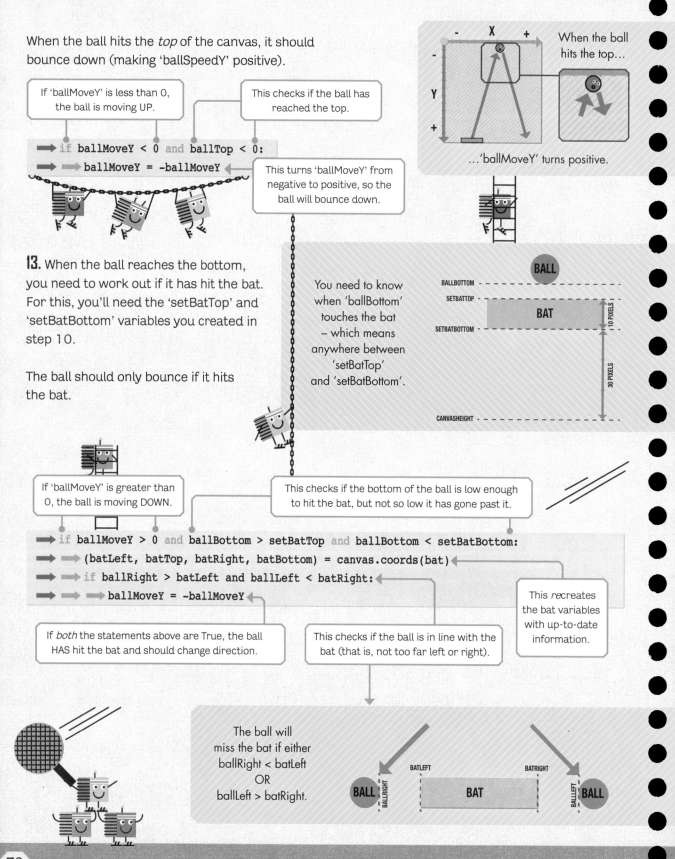

When the ball hits the *top* of the canvas, it should bounce down (making 'ballSpeedY' positive).

If 'ballMoveY' is less than 0, the ball is moving UP.

This checks if the ball has reached the top.

When the ball hits the top…

…'ballMoveY' turns positive.

```
if ballMoveY < 0 and ballTop < 0:
    ballMoveY = -ballMoveY
```

This turns 'ballMoveY' from negative to positive, so the ball will bounce down.

13. When the ball reaches the bottom, you need to work out if it has hit the bat. For this, you'll need the 'setBatTop' and 'setBatBottom' variables you created in step 10.

The ball should only bounce if it hits the bat.

You need to know when 'ballBottom' touches the bat – which means anywhere between 'setBatTop' and 'setBatBottom'.

BALL
BALLBOTTOM
SETBATTOP
BAT
SETBATBOTTOM
10 PIXELS
30 PIXELS
CANVASHEIGHT

If 'ballMoveY' is greater than 0, the ball is moving DOWN.

This checks if the bottom of the ball is low enough to hit the bat, but not so low it has gone past it.

```
if ballMoveY > 0 and ballBottom > setBatTop and ballBottom < setBatBottom:
    (batLeft, batTop, batRight, batBottom) = canvas.coords(bat)
    if ballRight > batLeft and ballLeft < batRight:
        ballMoveY = -ballMoveY
```

This *recreates* the bat variables with up-to-date information.

If *both* the statements above are True, the ball HAS hit the bat and should change direction.

This checks if the ball is in line with the bat (that is, not too far left or right).

The ball will miss the bat if either ballRight < batLeft OR ballLeft > batRight.

BATLEFT
BATRIGHT
BALL
BALLRIGHT
BAT
BALLLEFT
BALL

14. Finish the function by moving the ball.

```
➡ canvas.move(ball, ballMoveX, ballMoveY)
```

15. If the ball misses the bat and hits the bottom of the canvas, the game is over. Check for this with a new function, **check_game_over()**. You can ask if the player wants to play again with a pop-up message. A 'yes' will make the game reset, a 'no' will close the window.

MESSAGEBOX

Tkinter has a tool called **messagebox** that lets you create pop-up messages, also known as 'dialogue boxes'.

You can combine **messagebox** with functions to make specific kinds of dialogue box. For example, **askyesno()** adds clickable buttons for 'yes' and 'no'.

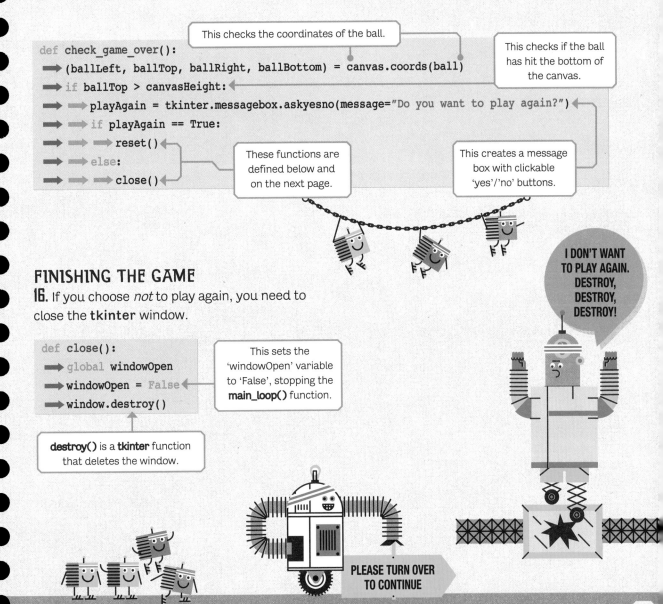

> This checks the coordinates of the ball.

> This checks if the ball has hit the bottom of the canvas.

```
def check_game_over():
➡    (ballLeft, ballTop, ballRight, ballBottom) = canvas.coords(ball)
➡    if ballTop > canvasHeight:
➡    ➡ playAgain = tkinter.messagebox.askyesno(message="Do you want to play again?")
➡    ➡ if playAgain == True:
➡    ➡ ➡ reset()
➡    ➡ else:
➡    ➡ ➡ close()
```

> These functions are defined below and on the next page.

> This creates a message box with clickable 'yes'/'no' buttons.

FINISHING THE GAME

16. If you choose *not* to play again, you need to close the **tkinter** window.

```
def close():
➡    global windowOpen
➡    windowOpen = False
➡    window.destroy()
```

> This sets the 'windowOpen' variable to 'False', stopping the **main_loop()** function.

destroy() is a **tkinter** function that deletes the window.

I DON'T WANT TO PLAY AGAIN. DESTROY, DESTROY, DESTROY!

PLEASE TURN OVER TO CONTINUE

17. To play again, you need to reset your variables.

```
def reset():
    global leftPressed, rightPressed
    global ballMoveX, ballMoveY
    leftPressed = 0
    rightPressed = 0
    ballMoveX = 4
    ballMoveY = -4
    canvas.coords(bat, 10, setBatTop, 50, setBatBottom)
    canvas.coords(ball, 20, setBatTop-10, 30, setBatTop)
```

You need to update the global variables you made in step 10.

Clear any previous key presses.

Reset the ball speed for both **x** and **y** movements.

Place the bat at the bottom of the screen, with the ball just above it.

18. You also need to make the game window react to mouse clicks and key presses. This will require two different link commands: **protocol** and **bind** (see box).

LINKING THINGS

It's often useful to link a function to a specific event, so your function is called whenever that event happens.

protocol links a function to a message from a **tkinter** window.

bind links a function to other events, such as a key press or release.

window means the **tkinter** window.

When a window is closed, it automatically sends out this message.

This line binds the act of pressing the **close** button [x] to the **close()** function which stops the main loop.

```
window.protocol("WM_DELETE_WINDOW", close)
window.bind("<KeyPress>", on_key_press)
window.bind("<KeyRelease>", on_key_release)
```

These lines bind the act of pressing and releasing a key to the functions you made in steps 5 and 6.

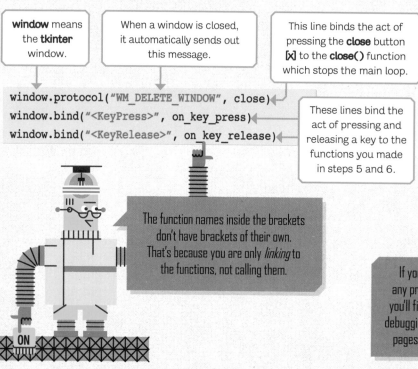

The function names inside the brackets don't have brackets of their own. That's because you are only *linking* to the functions, not calling them.

If you have any problems, you'll find some debugging tips on pages 88-89.

19. Finally, call the **reset()** and **main_loop()** functions to start the game.

```
reset()
main_loop()
```

This makes sure the game begins with all the right settings.

You've finished! Save and run the code to test it. How long can you keep the ball in the air?

KEEPING SCORE

If you want to keep track of how you're doing, you can add a score based on how many times you hit the ball.

1. To keep score, you need a new 'score' variable. Add this after the 'windowOpen' variable you made in step 4.

```
score = 0
```
← Set it to zero to start.

2. The score should go up by 1 each time the ball bounces off the bat. You can do this inside the **move_ball()** function.

```
def move_ball():
    global ballMoveX, ballMoveY, score
```
← Add 'score' to the end of this line.

```
        ballMoveY = -ballMoveY
        score = score + 1
    canvas.move(ball, ballMoveX, ballMoveY)
```
← Insert this line just above the final **move()** (from step 14) which makes the ball bounce off the bat.

3. Add a **print()** function to **check_game_over()**.

```
    if ballTop > canvasHeight:
        print("Your score was " + str(score))
```
← Add this line to display the score in the Shell window.

4. Finally, make sure the score goes back to zero when the game resets, by adding it to your **reset()** function.

```
def reset():
    global score
```
← Insert this line at the start, so you can access the global 'score' variable.

```
    score = 0
```
← Add this line at the end of the function.

Try the game now. You should see your score in the Shell window behind the canvas.

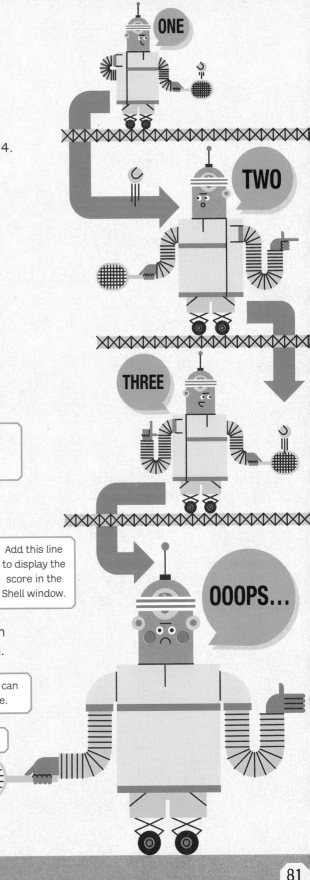

ONE

TWO

THREE

OOOPS...

GOING FASTER

If you like, you can try making the game more fun (read: harder) by making it gradually speed up.

1. You'll need another new variable to keep track of the bounces. Add this after your 'score' variable.

```
bounceCount = 0
```

2. In the **move_ball()** function, insert new code to make the 'bounceCount' go up with each bounce, and make the speed increase every fourth bounce.

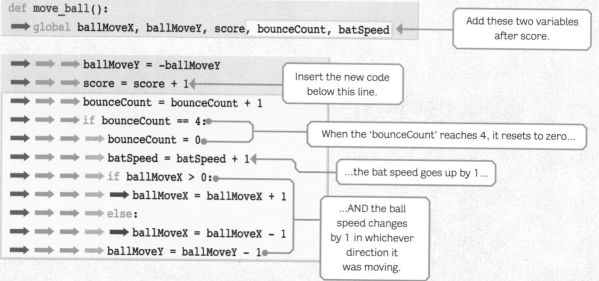

```
def move_ball():
    global ballMoveX, ballMoveY, score, bounceCount, batSpeed
```

Add these two variables after score.

```
        ballMoveY = -ballMoveY
        score = score + 1
        bounceCount = bounceCount + 1
        if bounceCount == 4:
            bounceCount = 0
            batSpeed = batSpeed + 1
            if ballMoveX > 0:
                ballMoveX = ballMoveX + 1
            else:
                ballMoveX = ballMoveX - 1
            ballMoveY = ballMoveY - 1
```

Insert the new code below this line.

When the 'bounceCount' reaches 4, it resets to zero...

...the bat speed goes up by 1...

...AND the ball speed changes by 1 in whichever direction it was moving.

3. Make 'bounceCount' and 'batSpeed' reset when the game restarts, by adding them to your **reset()** function.

```
def reset():
    global score, bounceCount, batSpeed

    bounceCount = 0
    batSpeed = 6
```

Add these lines at the end of the function.

4. Try the game now. It should gradually get faster. However, when the ball gets really fast, you may find it jumps through the bat. To fix this, you need to allow for its speed.

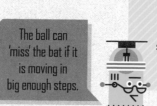

The ball can 'miss' the bat if it is moving in big enough steps.

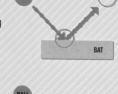

SLOW
When the ball is moving only a few pixels at a time, it hits the bat...

BALL
BAT

FAST
...but when the ball is moving a lot of pixels in each step, it can skip straight to the other side.

BALL
BAT

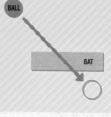

In your **move_ball()** function, delete this line:

> ➡ ➡ `if ballRight > batLeft and ballLeft < batRight:` ◄

DELETE the line that checked if the ball was in line with the bat.

When you have a long line of code, you can split it over two lines if you add brackets, like this.

and replace it with this:

```
➡ ➡ if ((ballMoveX > 0 and (ballRight+ballMoveX > batLeft and ballLeft < batRight)
    or ballSpeedX < 0 and (ballRight > batLeft and ballLeft+ballMoveX < batRight) )):
```

Here is the code for the whole program, with the extras highlighted like this.

```
import tkinter
import time
canvasWidth = 750
canvasHeight = 500
window = tkinter.Tk()
canvas = tkinter.Canvas(window, width=canvasWidth, height=canvasHeight, bg="dodgerblue4")
canvas.pack()
bat = canvas.create_rectangle(0, 0, 40, 10, fill="dark turquoise")
ball = canvas.create_oval(20, 0, 30, 10, fill="deep pink")
windowOpen = True
score = 0
bounceCount = 0
def main_loop():
    while windowOpen == True:
        move_bat()
        move_ball()
        window.update()
        time.sleep(0.02)
        if windowOpen == True:
            check_game_over()
leftPressed = 0
rightPressed = 0
def on_key_press(event):
    global leftPressed, rightPressed
    if event.keysym == "Left":
        leftPressed = 1
    elif event.keysym == "Right":
        rightPressed = 1
def on_key_release(event):
    global leftPressed, rightPressed
    if event.keysym == "Left":
        leftPressed = 0
    elif event.keysym == "Right":
        rightPressed = 0
batSpeed = 6
def move_bat():
    batMove = batSpeed*rightPressed - batSpeed*leftPressed
    (batLeft, batTop, batRight, batBottom) = canvas.coords(bat)
    if (batLeft > 0 or batMove > 0) and (batRight < canvasWidth or batMove < 0):
        canvas.move(bat, batMove, 0)
ballMoveX = 4
ballMoveY = -4
setBatTop = canvasHeight-40
setBatBottom = canvasHeight-30
def move_ball():
    global ballMoveX, ballMoveY, score, bounceCount, batSpeed
    (ballLeft, ballTop, ballRight, ballBottom) = canvas.coords(ball)
    if ballMoveX > 0 and ballRight > canvasWidth:
        ballMoveX = -ballMoveX
    if ballMoveX < 0 and ballLeft < 0:
        ballMoveX = -ballMoveX
    if ballMoveY < 0 and ballTop < 0:
        ballMoveY = -ballMoveY
```

THE CODE FOLLOWS ON FROM HERE...

...AND CONTINUES HERE

This is the original version – which you delete for 'Going faster'.

```
    if ballMoveY > 0 and ballBottom > setBatTop and ballBottom < setBatBottom:
        (batLeft, batTop, batRight, batBottom) = canvas.coords(bat)
        if ballRight > batLeft and ballLeft < batRight:
        if (ballMoveX > 0 and (ballRight+ballMoveX > batLeft and ballLeft < batRight)
        or ballMoveX < 0 and (ballRight > batLeft and ballLeft+ballMoveX < batRight)):
            ballMoveY = -ballMoveY
            score = score + 1
            bounceCount = bounceCount + 1
            if bounceCount == 4:
                bounceCount = 0
                batSpeed = batSpeed + 1
                if ballMoveX > 0:
                    ballMoveX = ballMoveX + 1
                else:
                    ballMoveX = ballMoveX - 1
                ballMoveY = ballMoveY - 1
    canvas.move(ball, ballMoveX, ballMoveY)
def check_game_over():
    (ballLeft, ballTop, ballRight, ballBottom) = canvas.coords(ball)
    if ballTop > canvasHeight:
        print("Your score was " + str(score))
        playAgain = tkinter.messagebox.askyesno(message="Do you want to play again?")
        if playAgain == True:
            reset()
        else:
            close()
def close():
    global windowOpen
    windowOpen = False
    window.destroy()
def reset():
    global score, bounceCount, batSpeed
    global leftPressed, rightPressed
    global ballMoveX, ballMoveY
    leftPressed = 0
    rightPressed = 0
    ballMoveX = 4
    ballMoveY = -4
    canvas.coords(bat, 10, setBatTop, 50, setBatBottom)
    canvas.coords(ball, 20, setBatTop-10, 30, setBatTop)
    score = 0
    bounceCount = 0
    batSpeed = 6
window.protocol("WM_DELETE_WINDOW", close)
window.bind("<KeyPress>", on_key_press)
window.bind("<KeyRelease>", on_key_release)
reset()
main_loop()
```

This the new version for 'Going faster'.

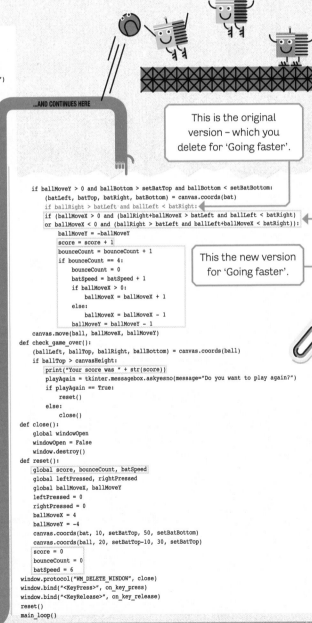

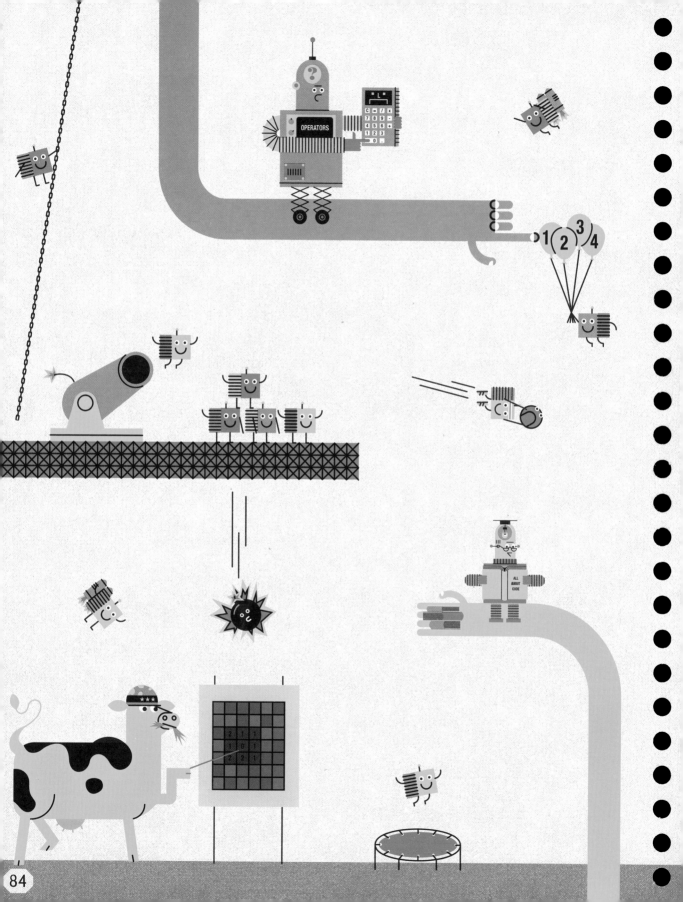

USEFUL STUFF

In this section you will find lots of general advice about Python, including debugging tips, a glossary of computer words, and how to read code written in Python.

For links to websites where you can discover all kinds of Python resources, including sites where you can upload and share your code, go to the Usborne Quicklinks website at **www.usborne.com/quicklinks** and enter the keyword: **python**. You'll also find downloadable Python files with finished, working code for the programs in this book.

DOWNLOADING PYTHON

If you don't already have Python on your computer,
you can download it for free. Here's how it works for a
recent Windows® computer (running Windows® Vista or newer).

1. First, check if your computer already has Python. Go to the 'Start' menu and click on 'All Programs'. If you see a program with the word Python or IDLE in it, or anything with the Python icon () then you have Python installed. Check that the version number begins with a 3, as earlier versions of Python won't run all the code in this book.

2. If you don't have it already, or if you have the wrong version, Python is available as a free download from the Python Software Foundation.
For a link, go to Usborne Quicklinks: **www.usborne.co.uk/quicklinks** and type in 'Python'.

3. Python comes in different versions, shown by different numbers after the name. This book uses version 3, so any version number beginning with a 3 will work. We recommend you download the latest version.

Click on the button to start the download.

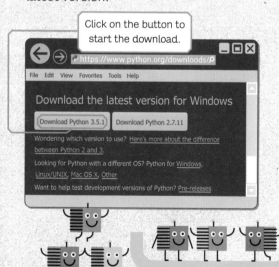

```
https://www.python.org/downloads/

File   Edit   View   Favorites   Tools   Help

Download the latest version for Windows

[ Download Python 3.5.1 ]   [ Download Python 2.7.11 ]

Wondering which version to use? Here's more about the difference
between Python 2 and 3.

Looking for Python with a different OS? Python for Windows,
Linux/UNIX, Mac OS X, Other

Want to help test development versions of Python? Pre-releases
```

4. The program will begin to download automatically. When it has finished, follow the instructions on screen to complete the installation. If you want to choose *where* to install it on your machine, choose the 'Customize installation' option, which will allow you to browse places on your computer. For example, you could save it in 'My Documents'.

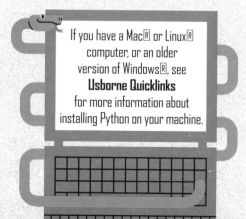

If you have a Mac® or Linux® computer, or an older version of Windows®, see **Usborne Quicklinks** for more information about installing Python on your machine.

MANAGING YOUR FILES

When you're using this book, or writing your own code,
it's a good idea to save your files regularly.

1. SAVING FILES

To save your code, go to the 'File' menu of the Code window and click 'Save As'. Type a name into the 'File name' box, then click 'Save'. As you write more code, *keep* saving it so you don't lose anything, especially if it's a long program.

NOOOO! I'VE LOST EVERYTHING!

Python files will default to saving in the same place on your computer as you installed the language. To save a file somewhere else, click on 'Save As' again and choose where you want to put it.

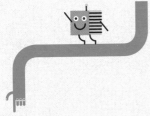

2. NAMING FILES

Python files always have **.py** after the name. Call each file something sensible, to help you find it again. If you're making changes, you can save separate versions by adding a number, e.g: **mygame_2.py**

3. OPENING FILES

Find the file you want and right-click on it, then select 'Edit with IDLE'. You can also open files by clicking on 'File', then 'Open', in the Python Shell or Code windows.

⚠ WARNING ⚠

If you open a file by double-clicking on the name, the computer will try to run it, but will usually fail or open it in the wrong window.

4. DELETING FILES

When you've finished a program, it's a good idea to delete old versions so your computer doesn't fill up with things you don't need. But double-check your version numbers so you don't delete something you still want.

5. LEAVING YOURSELF NOTES

You can leave **comments** in your code (created by putting a # at the start of a line) to leave notes for yourself – or anyone else looking at your programs. For example:

```
#This is the final version.
#Do not delete!
```

DEBUGGING

In coding, a spelling mistake or missing indent can break a program. It's totally normal to encounter a few bugs. Here are a few tips for finding and fixing some of the most common ones.

KNOW YOUR BUGS

There are three main types of error you can make in a program: **syntax**, **runtime** and **logic**. Some are easier to spot than others.

1. Syntax errors are the easiest to fix. It could be a spelling mistake, a missing colon at the end of an **if statement** or some other typing error. When one of these occurs, the program won't run. For example:

```
print("Hello world!
```
This code is missing a quote mark.

If you run this code in the Shell window, you'll get an error message, also in the Shell window, plus a red mark showing where the problem occurred.

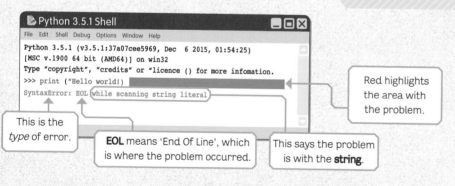

Red highlights the area with the problem.

This is the *type* of error.

EOL means 'End Of Line', which is where the problem occurred.

This says the problem is with the **string**.

If you run the same code as a saved program in the Code window, you'll get a pop-up message and see a red mark in the Code window.

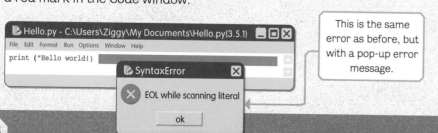

This is the same error as before, but with a pop-up error message.

QUICK BUG CHECKLIST

Some of the most common errors are the simplest to fix.

- **Spelling**: Computers can't recognize misspelled words. Check your spelling and capital letters.

- **Indents**: All the lines in the same block of code should have the same number of indents. After a colon, add an extra indent on the next line. At the end of a block, take away an indent.

- **Brackets and quote marks**: Make sure you always put brackets and quote marks in pairs. That goes for curved brackets (like this), square brackets [like this] and curvy brackets {like this}.

- **Colons**: check that each **conditional** statement has a colon **:** at the end, before an indented line.

LOOK UP!

If you can't spot a problem with the line that's given an error message, check the line above. Python might not realize there's a problem until the line *after* the bug.

2. Runtime errors are a little harder to spot. Runtime errors only show up when you run a program, for example, if you use a variable before it's defined, or forget to define it altogether.

```
print(variable1)
```

This won't work if 'variable1' hasn't been defined earlier in the code.

If there are multiple runtime errors, the program will break at the first one it reaches.

Runtime errors give an error message in the Shell window. For example, if you save the code above in the Code window and run it, you'll get this message in the Shell window:

This is the name of the program, and where it's saved.

```
Traceback (most recent call last):
  File "C:Users/Ziggy/My Documents changes.py", line 1, in <module>
    print(variable1)
NameError: name 'variable1' is not defined
```

This is the line number where the code broke.

This is the actual line of code.

This is the *type* of error.

This describes the problem ('variable1' hasn't been defined).

Some mistakes with numbers will cause runtime errors, such as trying to divide a number by 0, or trying to add numbers and strings together.

It's usually best to start looking at the LAST line of an error message and work your way back.

3. Logic errors are the hardest to spot, as the program will run and you won't get an error message. The program just won't do what it's supposed to. One cause of a logic error might be putting in the wrong values, or using the wrong operator (for example, > rather than <).

The code below is *meant* to print out the 5x table up to 12x5, but it doesn't because of a logic error.

```
for x in range(1,12):
    print(x,"x 5 =",x*5)
```

A range of 1-12 will only give 11 answers...

If you save and run the code, you won't get an error message, but you won't get the whole 5x table either – because the range is wrong.

```
1 x 5 = 5
2 x 5 = 10
3 x 5 = 15
4 x 5 = 20
5 x 5 = 25
6 x 5 = 30
7 x 5 = 35
8 x 5 = 40
9 x 5 = 45
10 x 5 = 50
11 x 5 = 55
```

Sometimes, it's easier to spot a bug if you add a **print()** function to your code, as you did on page 64.

WHICH WINDOW?

Python uses two main windows – the Shell window and the Code window. Here are the differences.

SHELL WINDOW

The **Shell** window is used for *running* code. You can also use it to write and test small pieces of code, but not save them. The Shell window opens automatically when you open IDLE, or when you run a program from the Code window.

CODE WINDOW

The **Code** window is used for *writing* code. Long programs should *always* be written in this window. It allows you to save and edit code. Use the 'File' menu in the Shell window and choose 'New file' to open the Code window.

THE WINDOW

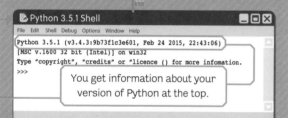

You get information about your version of Python at the top.

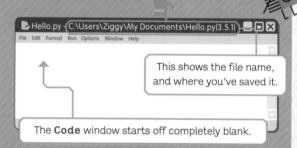

This shows the file name, and where you've saved it.

The **Code** window starts off completely blank.

WRITING CODE

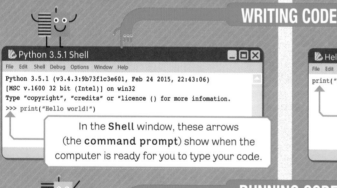

In the **Shell** window, these arrows (the **command prompt**) show when the computer is ready for you to type your code.

In the **Code** window, you write straight onto the page.

RUNNING CODE

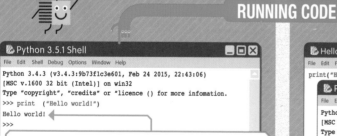

In the **Shell** window, when you finish a block of code and press return, the code runs immediately. The **output** appears in the same window.

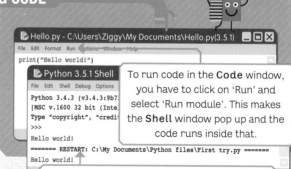

To run code in the **Code** window, you have to click on 'Run' and select 'Run module'. This makes the **Shell** window pop up and the code runs inside that.

If you run a program twice, you'll see RESTART in the Shell window the second time.

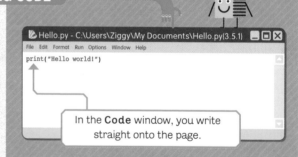

CODE AT A GLANCE

You can tell a lot about code just from looking at it – this page shows you how. If you want to check the meaning of any words, there is a glossary on the next page.

The brackets mean this is a **function**.

```
print()
```

The brackets are used to give information to the function.

Quotation marks mean this is a **string**.

```
print("Beep boop!")
```

An equals sign tells the computer to set the value of a **variable**, or create it if it doesn't exist.

```
bananas = 5
```

You can tell a lot from the text colours in **IDLE**:

- **Purple** means a built-in function.
- **Blue** means a function definition, or output from programs in the Shell window.
- **Green** means a string.
- **Orange** means a keyword.
- **Red** is used for error messages.
- **Black** means just about everything else!

Code with the same **indent** will run as a block – so these lines are both part of the same block.

```
def vshape():
    right(25)
    forward(50)
```

Colons link things together. A line ending in a colon will be followed by an indent, to show the new line belongs to the line above.

Square brackets show this is a **list**.

```
spacelist1 = ["rocket", "planet", "asteroid", "alien"]
```

The colons here link each **key** with its dictionary entry.

Curly brackets mean this is a **dictionary**.

```
powers = {"The Pigeon": "flight", "Cyborg": "controls machines"}
```

for loops are often used to repeat instructions a certain number of times.

```
for x in range(0,10):
    print(x)
```

Check inside the brackets to see the values, or **arguments**, given to the function.

while loops can be used to repeat instructions as long as a certain condition is met.

```
password = "password"
while password != "Open Sesame":
    password = input("Enter password.")
    if password == "Open Sesame":
        print("Correct!")
    else:
        print("Wrong! Try again.")
```

If and **else** tell the computer to react differently to different conditions.

Knowing how to read code makes it easier to understand programs and spot mistakes.

BUGS BEWARE!

GLOSSARY

animation A series of images shown one after another, to make it look as though things are moving.

argument In *Python*, a value that is given to a *function*. See also *parameter*.

binding In *Python*, linking a piece of *code* to a particular object on screen, or to an *event*.

block In *Python*, a section of *code* with the same *indent*, that runs as one unit.

Boolean expression A way of comparing two pieces of information using *Boolean logic*. See also *condition*.

Boolean logic A way of working things out, used by all *computers*, which involves breaking decisions down into simple yes/no questions.

Boolean value The status of a *Boolean expression*, which can be '*True*' or '*False*' (Yes or No).

brackets ( ) In maths and computing, brackets are used to group information together. In *Python*, they are also used with *functions* to contain the *parameters*.

branches The paths taken by a *conditional* depending on whether certain *conditions*

are *True* or *False*. If *True* the computer takes one branch of *code*, if *False* it takes another.

break A *command* that stops a *loop* from running.

bug An error in *code* which stops a *program* from working properly.

byte A unit used to measure amounts of *computer data*. See also *megabyte*.

calling a function In *Python*, asking the *computer* to run a particular *function*.

canvas In *Python*, a blank backdrop with *x* and *y* coordinates.

click Selecting something by clicking the mouse button (always the left mouse button, unless it says 'right-click').

code Instructions written in a *computer language*, which tell a *computer* what to do.

Code window In *Python*, the *window* used for writing, editing and saving long pieces of *code*.

coding Writing instructions for a *computer*.

command A piece of *code* that tells a *computer* to do something.

command prompt In *Python*, the arrows in the *Shell window* that show where to type your *code*.

comment Extra information for anyone reading the *code*. In *Python*, comments start with a '#' and aren't run as part of the *program*.

comparative operators In *Python*, *operators* are used to compare two pieces of information, such as '=='. See page 16.

computer A machine designed to follow instructions and process *data*; this is sometimes described as taking *input* and turning it into *output*.

computer language A language designed for *computers*, with a set word list and *syntax*; *Python* is one example.

computer logic The basic rules which all *computers* follow.

condition In computing, something which a *computer* must assess before making a decision.

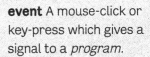

conditional Instructions which tell the *computer* to react differently to different *conditions*, such as '*if*' or '*else*'.

configuration A computing term for settings.

constant In computing, a piece of *data* which is fixed (as opposed to a *variable*).

coordinates A way of dividing an area into a grid and measuring distances, so you can find things by how far left/right (*x coordinate*) and up/down (*y coordinate*) they are.

cursor The flashing line which shows where your typing will appear on-screen. Also sometimes used as another name for the *mouse-pointer*.

data Information used by a *computer*. Any *data* that might change must be labelled – usually by creating *variables* or *lists*. A piece of *data* that does not change is sometimes described as a *constant*. See also, *string*.

debugging Fixing *code* to remove errors or *bugs*.

def In *Python*, a *keyword* used to create your own *function*.

define In *Python*, to create and assign a value or meaning to something, particularly *functions*.

delete To remove something from the *computer's* memory.

dictionary A way of storing information in *Python*. Each entry has a label, called a *key*, which can be used to retrieve the information.

double-click To click the left mouse button twice.

download To *save* something from the internet onto a *computer*.

drag In computing, to move an item while holding down a mouse button.

drop-down menu A *list* of options which appears when you *click*.

elif Short for 'else-if'. In *Python*, a *command* that comes into action for a specific path when an *if statement* is '*False*'.

ellipse A round or oval shape.

else In *Python*, a *command* that comes into action if *conditions* for an *if statement* and *elif statement* are '*False*'.

encrypt Encoding information so people can't decipher it.

event A mouse-click or key-press which gives a signal to a *program*.

exponent A number used to show how many times another number should be multiplied by itself, e.g. 3^4 means 3x3x3x3, where 4 is the exponent. Also known as a power.

False The value of a *Boolean expression* when a *condition* has not been met. Always written with a capital 'F' in *Python*. (See also *True*.)

file A set of information saved on a *computer*. Different types of *files* have different letters or *file extensions* at the end. See also *module*.

file extension The set of letters after the dot in a *file name*, which tells the *computer* what kind of information is in the *file*. For example .py is a *Python file*.

file name What you call a *file* when you *save* it on a *computer*.

float In computing, any number, including whole numbers and decimals.

flow chart A type of diagram which can be used to plan each step of a *program*.

folder A way of grouping different *computer files* when you *save* them.

for loop A section of code that makes the computer repeat a set of instructions a certain number of times.

function In *Python*, a section of *code* with a specific task, such as *print( )* or *input( )*.

function call In *Python*, when you use or *run* a function.

global In *Python*, a *keyword* that allows you to change a *global variable* within a *function*.

global variable In *Python*, a *variable*, created outside a *function*, which can be read by any *function*.

graphics Images on a *computer* screen.

GUI The buttons, icons and pictures that allow you to interact with a *computer*. Short for 'Graphical User Interface'.

icon In computing, a small picture which represents something, such as a *file* or *folder*.

IDLE A *Python program* that helps you write, edit, *save* and *run code*.

if A *keyword* used to test whether a *condition* is *True*. If it is, the *computer* follows the next instructions. If not, it skips them.

import In *Python*, a *keyword* that loads a *module* into your *program*.

in In *Python*, a *keyword* used to look in a particular *variable* or *range*.

indent Blank spaces at the beginning of a line. In *Python*, used to group lines of code together.

index In computing, the position of an item in a *list*, starting from 0.

input Information which you put into a *computer*.

input( ) In *Python*, a *function* that asks the user to enter some information.

int( ) In *Python*, a *function* that converts numbers or *strings* containing numbers into *integers*.

internet A huge network which allows *computers* around the world to communicate with each other.

integer A whole number.

keys In computing, labels given to items in a *dictionary*.

keyword Instruction word with a fixed, precise meaning for the *computer*, such as '*if*' in *Python*.

library In computing, a set of pre-written *code* you can *import* to use in your *programs*. See also *module*.

list A way of organising any number of pieces of information for a *computer*. Each item in the *list* has an *index* number, starting at 0.

loop A section of *code* that repeats. See also *for loop*, *nested loop* and *while loop*.

megabyte Just over one million (1,048,576) *bytes*.

menu In computing, a list of options, often opened by clicking a word at the top of a *window*.

module In *Python*, a *file* you can run (as in '*Run module*') or a *library* of *functions* you can *import* to use in your *programs*.

mouse-pointer The arrow you see on screen, which is controlled by moving the mouse.

nested loop A *loop* inside a loop.

operators Mathematical symbols, such as '+' , '-', '/' (divide) and '*' (multiply). (See page 9.) See also *comparative operators*.

output The results you get from a *computer*.

palette In computing, a display of available options (usually colours).

parameters In *Python*, the *variables* used by a *function*, which can be set when the function is called.

pixels The coloured dots which make up the picture on a screen.

print( ) In *Python*, a *function* that makes the *computer* display text on screen.

program A finished set of instructions in *computer language*, which tells a *computer* what to do.

Python The *computer language* used in this book.

random Not decided by a pattern or rule, so it's impossible to predict.

random module In *Python*, a *module* that generates *random* numbers.

randint( ) In *Python*, a *function* that generates a *random* number between the numbers or *parameters* given in the *brackets*.

range( ) In *Python*, a *function* that tells the *computer* to produce a list of numbers.

return value In *Python*, the result or value you get from a *function* when it *runs*.

right-click To click the right mouse button.

routine In computing, a named, reusable section of *code*.

run To set a *program* or section of *code* going.

save To store *computer files* so you can use them again later.

screen refresh When a *computer* updates the picture on screen.

Shell window In *Python*, a *window* used for running and testing *code*.

statement In computing, a section of *code* that describes an action to be carried out.

string In computing, a sequence of letters or numbers that the *computer* treats as characters (that is, not as a number).

syntax A way of setting out *code* so a *computer* will be able to understand it.

tkinter module In *Python*, a *library* used to create on-screen *graphics*, specifically for making *GUI*s.

True The value of a *Boolean expression* when a *condition* has been met. Always written with a capital 'T' in *Python*.

turtle module In *Python*, a *library* that can be used to create *graphics*. The *cursor* in the turtle *window* is also known as a 'turtle'.

upload To send *data* or *files* from your *computer* to the *internet*, usually so the contents can be used or viewed online.

variable A way of labelling information for a *computer*, so it can keep track of information that might change.

website A page (or group of pages) which you can look at on the *internet*.

window In computing, a framed area of the screen displaying information for a *program*.

while loop A *loop* that repeats as long as a certain *condition* is '*True*'.

x coordinate A number which decides how far left/right across a grid something appears.

y coordinate A number which decides how far up/down on a grid something appears.

INDEX

Edited by Rosie Dickins
Additional illustrations by Matt Preston
Code tested by Lara Bryan, Laura Cowan, Alice James,
Matthew Oldham and Thornhill Code Club